How We Got the Bible

Timothy Paul Jones, PhD

with

Garrick Bailey, Derek Brown, Samuel Emadi,
Elijah Hixson, and John David Morrison

HENDRICKSON
PUBLISHERS

ROSE
PUBLISHING

Peabody, Massachusetts

How We Got the Bible
© 2015 Timothy Paul Jones
Rose Publishing, LLC
P.O. Box 3473
Peabody, Massachusetts 01961-3473 USA
www.hendricksonrose.com

This book is published in association with Nappaland Literary Agency, an independent agency dedicated to publishing works that are: Authentic. Relevant. Eternal. Visit us on the web at Nappaland.com.

Cover design by Nancy Bishop, Layout design by Sergio Urquiza

Library of Congress Cataloging-in-Publication Data

Jones, Timothy P. (Timothy Paul)

  How we got the Bible / Timothy Paul Jones, PhD.

      pages cm

  Includes bibliographical references and index.

  ISBN 978-1-62862-216-4

1. Bible–History. I. Title.

  BS445.J66 2015

  220.1–dc23

                        2015016301

Printed in the United States of America
September 2017, 4th printing

How We Got the Bible

Contents

Chapter 1

What's So Special about the Bible?

- Inspiration
- Infallibility & Inerrancy
- Sufficiency

"Where's Jesus?" the little girl asked, and it was clear from her tear-rimmed eyes that she was very disappointed.[1]

It was the last day of Vacation Bible School at a tiny church in rural Missouri. The final fruit-flavored drinks and homemade cookies had been distributed, and the craft projects were glittered and glued. Now, twenty or so children clustered in the worship center for a closing assembly.

After leading a few songs, I told the children what I considered to be the most important message of the entire week. I talked to them about God's righteous wrath toward sin and the provision for peace that God has supplied through the death and resurrection of Jesus Christ.

"If you'd like to know Jesus," I said as the children's attention spans began to wane, "you can come back with me to a classroom to talk about it. I'll be glad to introduce you to Jesus."

One girl—an elementary student named Amy Jo—remained in the worship center after everyone else rushed outside. Amy Jo was always full of questions about God, and I'd been praying that she might become a believer in Jesus this week. She trotted beside me and another teacher down the hall to a Sunday School classroom that had been set aside for counseling.

Amy Jo seemed somewhat distraught when we walked into the room, but I assumed that the cause for her distress was conviction from the Holy Spirit. A few seconds later, it became apparent that her distress had nothing to do with the Spirit and everything to do with what she expected to find in the classroom—or, perhaps more precisely, who she expected to find.

"Where's Jesus?" she asked. "You said you'd be glad to introduce me to Jesus. I want to hear him talk to me."

"Well," I stammered a bit. "I didn't mean you'd talk to Jesus in person. I meant you could get to know Jesus by following him."

"But how can I follow Jesus if I never meet him and he never talks to me?" Amy Jo countered.

My attempt to share the truth about Jesus didn't end well that day, to say the least.

Amy Jo was disappointed that Jesus wasn't there to chat with her, and nothing I said seemed to help. She demanded nothing less than a personal visit from Jesus. Until Jesus appeared in that Sunday School classroom, she had no plans to believe anything I said about Jesus.

Why a Personal Visit from Jesus Wouldn't Make It Any Easier to Follow Him

Three years after that disappointing conclusion to a week of Vacation Bible School, Jesus still hadn't revealed himself in the flesh to Amy Jo. Still, God opened her heart to the truths that she heard from the Bible, and she trusted Jesus anyway. Now, nearly two decades later, Amy Jo and I share a laugh whenever we recall how she was convinced that Jesus resided in a Sunday School classroom in central Missouri. And yet, even as I smile at this memory, I can completely identify with Amy Jo's desire to hear a word from Jesus in the flesh.

After all, haven't you wished at some point in your life that Jesus would speak to you in person?

Maybe a hard conversation with an unbelieving friend raised one too many doubts about God's existence. Perhaps you were struggling to understand a recent tragedy, and you were convinced that a question-and-answer session with the Son of God could bring the clarity you needed. It could be that this yearning isn't a distant desire from your past; maybe you're wishing that God would speak to you in person right now.

If so, you're not alone.

We ache to hear God's voice because our souls were shaped to respond to God's voice. Even if we don't recognize it, we were created with a yearning for divine revelation. And yet, ever since the first human beings chose to challenge God's commands, no word from God—not even an audible message from the heavens—has been sufficient to keep us from rebelling against God's reign (Genesis 3:1–15).

✤ God spoke personally to Noah and provided him with plans for a ship to save humanity. And yet, this story of salvation ends with Noah waking up naked in his tent, nursing a hangover and cursing his son (Genesis 7:1; 9:20–27).

✢ Abraham glimpsed God's glorious presence and heard God promise that he would have a son. And yet, Abraham doubted God, lied about his wife, and tried to create an heir for himself with his wife's servant-girl (Genesis 12:1–18:21).

✢ God thundered from a mountain so that Abraham's descendants would obey him forever (Exodus 19:9). And yet, within a few weeks, these recipients of divine revelation were dancing in the shadow of an idol (Exodus 32:1–35).

The little girl in Vacation Bible School so many years ago was convinced that it would be easier to follow God if only he would speak to her in person. Yet the experiences of God's people demonstrate clearly that divine epiphanies don't make it any easier to obey. The positive effect of these revelations is fleeting at best.

It's no wonder then that, thousands of years ago, God called particular people to record his words in a way that would be stable and available even after the memories of his miraculous works faded. God began to inspire a book.

This God-inspired book wasn't an afterthought or an accident! Eternal eons before God created darkness and light, God had already decided that he would reveal his kingdom not only through spoken words but also through written words. The Bible that you possess today is the perfect product of this eternal plan (Psalm 119:89). The purpose of the book you're reading right now is to deepen your trust in the Bible by helping you to understand how God's written revelation made the journey from the mind of God to the sixty-six texts in your Bible today.

Where the Bible Came From

God is revealing his truth to all people at every moment through his creation (Romans 1:18–20)—but God also chooses to reveal himself in particular ways to particular people. Beginning at least as early as Moses, God began to unveil his truth in written propositions. These written words were so precious that no one was ever to change them (Deuteronomy 4:2; 12:32).

In the centuries that followed God's initial written revelation, inspired men and women continued to write "as they were moved by the Holy Spirit" (2 Peter 1:21). Some chronicled historical events. Others penned poems and proverbs and songs. Still others wrote prophecies that called people to return to God's reign over their lives.

But these books possessed a purpose far greater than merely recording God's work in the lives of ancient people!

Throughout all those centuries of revelation, God was inspiring the words of Scripture in such a way that the writers were revealing a greater message than they themselves could clearly see.[2] Every written word of the Old Testament highlighted humanity's need for a living Word who was yet to come (John 5:39). Taken together, all the prophecies of the Old Testament testified in perfect harmony that it was only through faith in a future Messiah that anyone's sins could be forgiven (Acts 10:43). This Messiah would be God's greatest revelation, the living Word of God sent to earth in human flesh (John 1:1–18).

The Word Became Flesh

When it was time to send this Word to earth, God announced his arrival through priests and prophets, angels and starry signs splashed across the eastern sky (Matthew 1:20–21; 2:2; Luke 1:11–18, 26–38, 67–80; 2:8–15, 25–38; 7:24–28). The living Word of God grew into adulthood and sacrificed his life on a cross, embracing God's wrath in place of everyone who would trust in him. After he rose to life on the third day, this same Word filled his people's hearts with his Spirit and empowered them to proclaim his kingdom throughout the world (Matthew 28:18–20; John 14:16–26; Acts 1:8).

But God's revelation didn't stop with the living Word or even with his presence in the lives of his people!

As the message of Jesus multiplied throughout the world, God began to inspire new writings that preserved the truth about Jesus and revealed how to live in his kingdom. During the first decades that followed the resurrection of Jesus, Christians memorized eyewitness accounts about Jesus and wrote letters that applied Jesus' teachings in the lives of his followers. Soon, these spoken testimonies about Jesus began to be brought together with the teachings of Jesus to produce four "Gospels" written by Matthew, Mark, Luke, and John.

Christians throughout the first-century churches treated texts connected to apostles and eyewitnesses of Jesus as inspired guides for their lives. Since every authoritative text in the churches had to be linked somehow to an eyewitness, written revelations ended as the first-century eyewitnesses and their associates passed away.

Nearly 2,000 years later, these God-inspired revelations from ancient Israelites and Christ-commissioned eyewitnesses remain the main means that God uses to unveil his truth to humanity. Jesus is the one Word of God, but we also rightly refer to these writings—now gathered together into the book we know as "the Bible"—as "the Word of God." We refer to the Bible as God's Word because this one book and only this book bears perfect witness to God's living Word, Jesus Christ.

Where Did the Word "Bible" Come From?

The English word "Bible" comes from the Latin word *biblia* ("books"), which descended from a Greek word, *byblos*. The Greek *byblos* described papyrus—an ancient writing material made from reeds that grow along the Nile River in Egypt.[3] Ancient people stitched or pasted together pieces of papyri and rolled them to create scrolls.

No later than the first century, papyri and other writing materials began to be stacked and folded to form *codexes* (or, *codices*), the predecessors of modern books. As codexes grew in popularity, the meaning of *biblia* broadened to include both scrolls and codexes.[4] The Jewish people already used the word *biblia* to describe their holy writings; early Christians quickly picked up the same word to refer to the Hebrew Scriptures and Christian Scriptures together.[5] Ever since that time, the word "Bible"—from the Latin word for "books"—has meant the collection of texts that comprise the sacred writings of the Jewish and Christian faiths. A pastor named Tertullian used the terms "Old Testament" and "New Testament" in the early third century to distinguish the Hebrew Scriptures and the Christian Scriptures.[6]

What the Bible *Is*

The Bible is made up of sixty-six Spirit-inspired writings penned by many people "at many times and in many ways" over many centuries (Hebrews 1:1). These words from God were given for the purpose of pointing fallen humanity to Jesus, the crucified and risen King. To gain an adequate understanding of the Bible, however, we must move beyond knowing merely what the Bible is *made of*. In a fantasy novel by C. S. Lewis, a character named Eustace looks at a star and points out, "In our world ... a star *is* a huge ball of flaming gas." Another individual—who happens to be a retired star—corrects him by saying, "That is not what a star is, but only what it is *made of*."[7] To understand the stars in the world of Narnia, Eustace needed to know not only what stars were *made of* but also what they *were*. Likewise, to understand the nature of Scripture, we need to explore not only what the Bible is *made of* but also what the Bible *is*.

> Because every word of Scripture is breathed out by God, the Bible stands as the full and final authority for God's people.

According to the testimony of Scripture and declarations of faith that have been confessed throughout the church's history, the Bible is:

✤ inspired,

✤ inerrant and infallible, and

✤ sufficient.

Let's take a look together at each of these vital characteristics of Scripture.

Inspiration: The Bible Is God-Breathed

"All Scripture," the apostle Paul wrote to his protégé Timothy, "is inspired by God and profitable for teaching, for reproof, for correction, for training in righteousness so that the man of God may be adequate, equipped for every good work" (2 Timothy 3:16–17). A more accurate rendering of the phrase "inspired by God" might be "God-breathed."[8] If Scripture is "God-breathed," that means the words of Scripture came to us from the innermost essence of God himself. Moses and the prophets knew this and declared that they were writing God's own words (see, for examples, Exodus 17:14; Jeremiah 1:9; Ezekiel 1:2; Hosea 1:1). Jesus agreed with their assessment and described the words of Scripture as words from God himself (Matthew 19:4–5; Mark 12:36).[9]

Notice that God did not merely inspire the *authors* of Scripture! God inspired the *text itself*. If Paul had thought the authors were inspired but not the text, Paul could have written something like this to Timothy: "Everyone who wrote Scripture was inspired by God." But that's not at all what Paul said or thought! Paul said that "all Scripture is God-breathed" (2 Timothy 3:16) because he believed that the very words of Scripture originated in God.

So what specific documents did Paul have in mind when he dictated the word "Scripture" and described these texts as "God-breathed"?

Paul's words pointed primarily to the Old Testament. After all, when Paul wrote his second letter to Timothy, some New Testament texts weren't even finished! Yet, even when Paul wrote this letter, Christians were already aware that "Scripture" included not only the Old Testament but also the words of believers who had seen the risen Jesus and close associates of these eyewitnesses. Two biblical texts make it clear that, by the mid-first century, Christians were already treating New Testament writings as Scripture:

✣ In Paul's first letter to Timothy, Paul identified words spoken by Jesus that became part of Luke's Gospel as "Scripture" (compare Luke 10:7 with 1 Timothy 5:18).

Verbal-Plenary Inspiration

For centuries, Bible-believing Christians have accepted two important truths about the inspiration of Scripture:

- Verbal inspiration (Latin *verbum*, "word")— God's inspiration extends to the very words of Scripture.
- Plenary inspiration (Latin *plenus*, "full")— Every part of the Bible is fully inspired, not merely the parts that have to do with salvation and our spiritual lives.

Verbal-plenary inspiration does *not* mean that God turned writers into robots, controlled from heaven through a cosmic keyboard. The biblical authors used their own free expressions, and God providentially guided their lives so that they would choose the words that conveyed his truth.

✤ Shortly after Paul wrote his second letter to Timothy, Simon Peter referred to Paul's letters as "Scripture" (2 Peter 3:16).

Even while the texts in the New Testament were being penned and assembled, early Christians knew that writings linked to believers commissioned by the risen Lord Jesus carried the same authority as the Old Testament Scriptures.

Because every word of Scripture is breathed out by God, the Bible stands as the full and final authority for God's people. The Bible in its entirety is the Creator's message to his creatures, the King's edict to his citizens, and the Spirit's tool for transforming his people. Church traditions, creeds, and confessions of faith can be useful, but they can never claim authority equal to God's inspired Word.

Infallibility and Inerrancy: The Bible Is Error-Free

Titus was a young pastor on an island where the inhabitants were well-known for their dishonesty (Titus 1:12). Perhaps that's why Paul opened his letter to Titus with the simple reminder that "God ... does not lie" (Titus 1:2). I lie, you lie—but God never lies (Romans 3:4).

With that in mind, let's ask ourselves a crucial question: If all Scripture is God-breathed and if God never lies, what does that tell us about the reliability of Scripture?[10]

The word "infallibility" comes from a Latin word that meant "unable to deceive" or "not liable to err." When we say that the Bible is "infallible," what we mean is that Scripture tells the truth and never deceives us.

Throughout history, faithful Christians have agreed that, if God can't lie, his written revelation can't lie either. Our trust in the truthfulness of Scripture is rooted in our belief in the trustworthy character of God. A broad range of words and phrases have been used in different eras to describe the truthfulness of Scripture. One of the most important of these terms is "infallibility." The word "infallibility" comes from a Latin word that meant "unable to deceive" or "not liable to err." When we say that the Bible is "infallible," what we mean is that Scripture tells the truth and never deceives us. Another, more recent term to describe the truthfulness of Scripture is "inerrant," a word that simply means "not in error."[11]

Error-prone human beings put the Scriptures together, but God was at work among these inspired authors and editors, preventing them from introducing any errors into his written revelation. That's why we can trust that "when all the facts are known, the Scriptures ... properly interpreted will be shown to be wholly true in everything they affirm."[12] Inerrancy does not require Scripture to be scientifically precise, and inerrancy certainly doesn't rule out figurative language or numeric estimates in the Bible. "Scripture is inerrant, not in the sense of being absolutely precise by modern standards, but in the sense of making good its claims and achieving that measure of focused truth at which its authors aimed."[13] For example:

✤ In 1 Kings 7:23, a circular pool in the temple is described as "ten cubits from rim to rim" and "thirty cubits ... around." A circular pool ten cubits in diameter would actually be slightly larger than thirty cubits around. Yet the biblical author didn't make an error because mathematical precision wasn't his purpose. The purpose of this text was simply to describe an object that Solomon's metalworkers made, and the author used rounded numbers in his description.

✤ When an ancient chronicler of Israel's history recorded the demise of 18,000 Edomites (2 Samuel 8:13), this author probably wasn't taking a precise census of how many Edomites died; he was providing a rounded figure based on the information he possessed. And so, if the exact death toll numbered a thousand or two higher or lower than the number recorded, that's not an error; it's an estimate.

✤ When Scripture says "the sun rose," the biblical authors were describing daybreak from an earth-dweller's perspective (Genesis 32:31; Jonah 4:8); these authors didn't err anymore than weather reporters today are mistaken when they refer to "sunrise" and "sunset" on the morning news.[14]

God revealed his message through human authors who recorded truthful testimony in different genres and styles of writing. To whatever extent precision was necessary to express God's truth, Scripture tells the truth with precision.[15]

Did the early church leaders believe in the inerrancy of Scripture?

The earliest Christians never used the words "inerrancy" and "infallibility." However, from the earliest stages of Christian history, faithful church leaders treated Scripture as God's inerrant and infallible revelation.

- "You have searched the Scriptures, which are true and given by the Holy Spirit. You know that nothing unrighteous or counterfeit is written in them." —Clement of Rome, first century[16]

- "All Scripture, which has been given to us by God, [is] perfectly consistent. The parables harmonize with the passages that are plain; and statements with a clearer meaning serve to explain the parables."—Irenaeus of Lyons, second century[17]

- "I am entirely convinced that no Scripture contradicts another." —Justin Martyr, second century[18]

- "The statements of Holy Scripture will never contradict the truth."—Tertullian of Carthage, third century[19]

- "It is the opinion of some that the Scriptures do not agree or that the God who gave them is false. But there is no disagreement at all. Far from it! The Father, who is truth, cannot lie."—Athanasius of Alexandria, fourth century[20]

- "I have learned to give respect and honor to the canonical books of Scripture. Regarding these books alone, I most firmly believe that their authors were completely free from error. If in these writings I am confused by anything which appears to me opposed to the truth, I do not hesitate to suppose that either the manuscript is faulty, or the translator has not caught the meaning of what was said, or I myself have failed to understand it."—Augustine of Hippo, fifth century[21]

Sufficient: The Bible Is Enough

So far, we've learned that the Bible is God-breathed and error-free—but is the Bible enough?

That's one aspect of the challenge that the little girl was facing in that Sunday School classroom so many years ago. Before she was willing to trust Jesus, Amy Jo wanted something more than the Word that she heard in the Scriptures—a personal chit-chat with Jesus, in her particular case. In time, she recognized that what the Bible provided was enough for her to trust God. In theological terms, what she recognized was the *sufficiency of Scripture*.

Throughout history, Christians have treated Scripture as sufficient in two senses: First and foremost, Scripture provides enough knowledge for us to find God's truth and to live in fellowship with him. Second, Scripture has been copied with enough accuracy to preserve God's truth.

(1) Scripture provides us with sufficient knowledge to trust God and to live in fellowship with him. The biblical texts, as they were originally written, contain every truth that's needed for us to be saved and to follow our Savior. "Never in church history has God added to the teachings or commands of Scripture. … Scripture is sufficient to equip us for 'every good work'" (2 Timothy 3:15–16).[22]

The Meaning of Inerrancy

In 1978, more than 300 Christian leaders—including John MacArthur, R. C. Sproul, Francis Schaeffer, J. I. Packer, and Carl F. H. Henry—gathered in Chicago. There, they developed a statement that clarified the meaning and implications of biblical inerrancy.

Here are three key affirmations and denials from the Chicago Statement on Biblical Inerrancy:

- "We affirm that the Holy Scriptures are to be received as the authoritative Word of God. We deny that the Scriptures receive their authority from the Church, tradition, or any other human source."
- "We affirm that Scripture in its entirety is inerrant, being free from all falsehood, fraud, or deceit. We deny that biblical infallibility and inerrancy are limited to spiritual, religious or redemptive themes, exclusive of assertions in the fields of history and science."
- "We affirm that Scripture, having been given by divine inspiration, is infallible, so that, far from misleading us, it is true and reliable in all matters it addresses. We deny that it is possible for the Bible to be at the same time infallible and errant in its assertions. Infallibility and inerrancy may be distinguished, but not separated."[23]

The sufficiency of Scripture doesn't mean, of course, that the Bible includes every truth we will ever need to complete every task in our lives! Scripture doesn't provide us with much information when it comes to installing ceramic tile or conjugating German verbs, for example, and performing brain surgery based only on information found in the Bible is likely to end badly for everyone. And so, Scripture doesn't *reveal* all things. Instead, Scripture is sufficient to show us *how to do* all things for the glory of God, with the mind of Christ, through the power of the Holy Spirit (Romans 15:13; 1 Corinthians 10:31; Philippians 2:5).

(2) Scripture survives in texts that were copied with sufficient accuracy to preserve God's truth. For nearly a millennium and a half, the biblical texts were copied by hand. There were no printing presses, no copy machines, no dictation devices, no word processors with autocorrect features—only ordinary scribes copying texts phrase by phrase from piles of parchment and papyrus. Over the centuries, some of these scribes made mistakes. Most times, scribes merely missed or misspelled a word or two in a particular verse. Other times, when one scribe was reading a text aloud and others were writing what was said, scribes misheard words. Once in a while, scribes switched words or added phrases to emphasize truths that were tied to hot topics in their day. And so, copying variants can be found throughout the ancient biblical manuscripts.

This fact does not, however, mean that the Bible somehow ceases to be infallible or inerrant. Inerrancy and infallibility refer to each biblical text *as it was originally composed*—not to every copy made later.[24] And, truth be told, so many copies of Scripture have survived—more than any other ancient document!—that it's almost always possible to reconstruct the precise wording of the original texts. In the minuscule number of instances where questions about original wordings remain, not one textual difference affects anything that we believe about God or his work in the world. The copies of Scripture that survive today preserve enough of the original text to convey the original message that God inspired.[25]

This vast trove of highly reliable texts shouldn't surprise us. God himself promised that he would protect and preserve his message (Psalm 119:89; Isaiah 40:8; Matthew 5:18; Mark 13:31). Thousands of manuscripts and textual fragments testify together that this promise has been kept. That's why it's entirely appropriate for us to treat our Bible today as a trustworthy record of God's written revelation.

Why God Preserved His Word

God's goal in preserving his Word was far greater than merely multiplying people's knowledge or improving their morals. The Bible "is not an inspired book of moralisms or a book of virtues; it is, from cover to cover, a book about the glory of God in Jesus Christ through the redemption of his people who will dwell in the kingdom of Christ forever."[26] The center-point of Scripture is Jesus Christ himself, and the goal of the storyline of Scripture is his kingdom.

> Scripture is inerrant in its inspiration, sufficient in its preservation, and dependent on interpretation and illumination for its application.

So how can we make certain that Scripture transforms us and turns us toward Christ? That requires both *interpretation* and *illumination*.

Seeking the Right Interpretation

Since first-century Christians saw Scripture as a word from Jesus Christ himself, they placed a high priority on rightly interpreting Scripture. The New Testament was still being written when Paul warned Timothy to watch carefully how he interpreted Scripture (1 Timothy 4:11–16). In a later letter, Paul returned to this same point and reminded his protégé to prioritize "rightly handling the word of truth" (2 Timothy 2:15).

So how do we rightly interpret Scripture today? We begin by studying each text in its historical context. If we're reading Daniel, for example, we need to discover how the exiled Israelites who first received this book understood Daniel's Spirit-

How can we know whether our application of a text is a result of the Spirit's illumination?

The Holy Spirit is the Spirit of truth; any truth that comes from the Spirit originates with the Father and exalts the Son (John 15:26; 16:12–13). The Spirit of truth will never illumine an application of the text of Scripture that contradicts sound interpretation of the text.

inspired dreams. When studying Isaiah, it's important to ask, "How would Isaiah's first readers have interpreted this text?" But we never stop there, because Jesus and the apostles never stopped there! Jesus and the apostles understood that Jesus himself "is the focus of every single word of the Bible. Every verse of Scripture finds its fulfillment in him, and every story in the Bible ends with him."[27] That's why we look at each part of the Bible in the context of the whole Bible, believing that every part of Scripture connects with other parts of Scripture to reveal Jesus and his kingdom (Luke 24:44; Acts 10:43).

Receiving the Spirit's Illumination

Even when we think we're interpreting Scripture rightly, it's entirely possible to miss the message of Jesus. Remember the first-century Jewish theologians who encountered Jesus in the flesh? They were world-class experts when it came to interpreting the Bible, but they completely missed the point of the Scriptures (John 5:39). So will we, until the Holy Spirit shows us how to respond to God's Word (John 14:26; 16:12–15; 1 Corinthians 2:10–13; 2 Corinthians 3:14–18). Unless the Spirit is at work within us, we may hear the words of Scripture, but we will never understand Scripture rightly or apply the message in our lives (James 1:22–2:26).

God's Word-revealing work is known as *illumination*. "Without the illumination of the Spirit," a French pastor named John Calvin once commented, "the Word will have no effect."[28] Reading the Bible without the Spirit is like trying to read a map in a cave; without some source of light, the map may be right in front of you, but you will never figure out which way to go. As we read and interpret Scripture, the Spirit shows us how the Word should reshape our lives. We respond to this illumination by loving God more fully and by resting more deeply in the grace that he has provided in Jesus.

Where to Go First If You Want to Hear a Word from Jesus

"Where's Jesus?" the little girl asked as she surveyed the empty classroom. "I want to hear him talk to me."

Despite this child's earnest expectations, the current location of God the Son is not in a Sunday School classroom in central Missouri; he's with the Father in a position of heavenly honor (Luke 22:69; Acts 2:33; 5:31; 7:55–56). And yet, the fact that Jesus Christ isn't physically present among us doesn't mean we can't hear from him! The prophets and apostles wrote what they wrote in Scripture because "the Spirit of Christ" declared it (1 Peter 1:11). "Ignorance of Scripture is," in the words of the fifth-century church father Jerome, "ignorance of Christ."[29]

What this means for our daily lives is that, if we yearn for a word from Jesus, the solution isn't a personal trip into the heavens or an ecstatic vision on the earth. The answer isn't even found by waiting for Jesus in a Sunday School classroom!

If you long for Jesus to speak to you, open your Bible.

Drink deeply from the truths you find there.

Read these texts in the context of faithful Christians gathered in community.

Meditate on these words in their manifold beauty, and receive them as the very words of God—because that is what they are.

The Word of God has been made flesh for us in Jesus Christ, written for us in Holy Scripture, and proclaimed among us whenever the Scripture are faithfully taught. You never need to wonder what God might say is true if he showed up in the center of our circumstances. God has already embraced the circumstances of this world once and for all in the flesh of Jesus Christ, and he has made his truth accessible to you in the text of Scripture.

"The Bible is the God-given means through which we know who Jesus is. Take the Bible away, diminish it or water it down, and you are free to invent a Jesus just a little bit different from the Jesus who is hidden in the Old Testament and revealed in the New. We live under Scripture because that is the way we live under the authority of God that has been vested in Jesus the Messiah, the Lord."
—N. T. Wright[30]

The Unity of Scripture

At least forty human authors composed the Bible over the span of more than 1,000 years, but this doesn't mean that the Bible is fragmented or haphazard. The sixty-six books of Scripture intertwine to tell a single glorious story—the story of God's creation, humanity's sin, and God's provision for the redemption of his people through Jesus Christ. God's covenants with humanity throughout the Scriptures are the spine that ties this storyline together.[31]

How We Got the Old Testament

Has it ever seemed to you that the New Testament and the Old Testament don't fit together very well?

Maybe it feels as if the Old Testament caught God on a particularly grumpy Monday morning, whereas the New Testament was inspired on a sunny weekend after a few cups of coffee and a round of golf. Perhaps it even seems like the two testaments are too different to have come from the same God.

Once upon a time, that's precisely how the Bible seemed to a certain pastor's son. In time, the tension this man sensed between the testaments erupted into a new religious movement.

A Mutilated Bible and Multiple Gods

From the time he was a child, this pastor's son had heard the words of the Old and New Testaments read alongside each other. As a young man, he made a fortune building boats and donated millions to the megachurch where he'd become a member. Then, sometime in middle adulthood, this same man began to question the beliefs he'd received as a child.

The pastor's son became obsessed with the differences between the two testaments, and he concluded that the Old Testament described a completely different deity from the New Testament. The God who created the cosmos was not—according to this new point of view—the same God who sent Jesus to earth.

Once the pastor's son arrived at this conclusion, he began condensing Scripture to fit his new beliefs. First, he cut out the entire Old Testament, since he saw the Old Testament as the errant revelation of a lesser god. Then, he slashed everything out of his New Testament except Luke's Gospel and ten of Paul's letters. With only eleven texts left, learning the books of the Bible in his Sunday School class suddenly became a far simpler task!

Yet even these mutilations weren't enough to accommodate his new beliefs. To finalize his revisions, he trimmed every hint of God's revelation to Israel from Luke's Gospel and Paul's letters. When he was finished, not even the slightest shred or shadow of the Old Testament remained in his Bible.

Despite pleas from prominent Christian leaders, the preacher's son refused to stop proclaiming two separate gods and a stripped-down Bible. His church disfellowshipped him—but even that didn't slow him down. Soon, he was traveling to other parts of the world, trying to convince Christians to mutilate their Bibles and modify their beliefs to accommodate his dynamic duo of divinities. In the end, his views were condemned, and his followers faded—but not before thousands of people embraced his skewed thinking about the Bible.

So when did this preacher's son proclaim these problematic beliefs?

Was it in the early nineteenth century, around the same time that Joseph Smith declared that his *Book of Mormon* represented a new revelation from God? Maybe it was during the late nineteenth and early twentieth centuries when movements like the Christian Scientists were claiming that physical affliction was an illusion? Or perhaps it was in the early twenty-first century when books like *The Da Vinci Code* hit the bestseller lists and renewed interest in ancient heresies?

Not even close.

The name of the preacher's son was Marcion of Pontus, and Marcion began proclaiming his ideas in the first half of the second century AD—less than a generation after the death of the last apostle! When Marcion was born in northern Asia Minor, the apostle John was most likely still alive and preaching in western Asia Minor.

For a short time in the second century, "Marcionism" became wildly popular in certain regions of the Roman Empire. It wasn't long, however, before Christians recognized Marcionism as heresy and rejected Marcion's claims about God and the Bible. Still, the shipbuilder from Pontus raised some worthwhile questions about the Bible—questions that people still ask today.

Do Christians Need the Old Testament?

Even though we rightly reject Marcion's claim that different deities delivered the Old and New Testaments, it's easy to wonder whether Christians really need the Old Testament. Might it be possible to disregard the Old Testament without diminishing our faith in Jesus? Put another way, is the story of Israel necessary to understand the story of Jesus Christ?

The best way to find the answer is simply by listening to the teachings of Jesus.

A century before Marcion began hawking his heresies in Asia Minor and Rome, Jesus treated the whole Old Testament as "the word of God" (Mark 7:13; see also Matthew 22:31–32; John 10:35). Jesus criticized the religious leaders' misuse of his Father's words—but he never corrected or contradicted the Old Testament laws and prophecies. Instead, he fulfilled them, and he treated them as the unerring revelation of his Father's will. The earliest Christians revered the Old Testament as God's Word because their Savior had recognized the Old Testament as God's Word. That's why churches in the second century rightly and rapidly rejected Marcion's removal of the Old Testament from his Bible.

Sure, there are discontinuities between the Old Testament and the New Testament. That's because God's fulfillment of his promises in Jesus Christ inaugurated the kingdom that the Old Testament merely foreshadowed. But there's also unmistakable continuity between the two testaments, because the same God was fulfilling the same promises in both testaments.[1] The Creator God who inspired the Old Testament was also the heavenly Father who sent his Son to be the Savior of the world.

"Marcion ... is cloudier than the fog, ... more brittle than the ice, more treacherous than the Danube River, more precipitous than the Caucasus Mountains. ... Could any rodent consume more than this man who now gnaws away the Gospels? ... His followers can't deny that his faith once agreed with ours. His own letter proves it! ... Now, this man from Pontus presents us with double deities, two clashing rocks on which he shipwrecks himself. ... But a single lamp only looks double to the bleary-eyed. ... If God is not one God, he is no god at all."
—Tertullian of Carthage, late second century[2]

Chapter 2

How Did the Old Testament Get from God to You?

- Old Testament Writers
- Preserving Ancient Scripture
- The Dead Sea Scrolls

S ome stories simply can't be started in the middle. Take the *Star Wars* saga, for example. When you decide it's time to introduce your children to *Star Wars,* you might start with *Episode I: The Phantom Menace* or with the original classic film from 1977—but you certainly wouldn't start with the climactic scene in *Episode VI: Return of the Jedi* when the Emperor is defeated and Anakin Skywalker is redeemed! If you tried such a tactic, your child would be completely confused. Who are the Jedi? What is the Force? How did Anakin Skywalker become Darth Vader, and why didn't he know that both Luke and Leia were his children?

Star Wars can't be introduced so late in the saga without making a mess of the storyline.

It's that way with lots of great books and films. If you read *The Last Battle* in *The Chronicles of Narnia* without first working through *The Lion, the Witch, and the Wardrobe* and a couple of the other chronicles, the final volume in the series won't be nearly as meaningful. The revolution that Katniss Everdeen leads in *Mockingjay* makes no sense apart from *The Hunger Games,* and you will never comprehend *The Lord of the Rings* saga if you only read *Return of the King.*

It's the same way when it comes to the storyline of Scripture. The Old Testament is "'Part One' of a unique two-part epic."[1] We can't cut out the first part of this epic without mutilating the whole saga.

> *The Story of Jesus … makes sense only as it follows and completes the Story of Israel. … The apostles' gospel was the Story of Jesus resolving the Story of Israel. The texts the apostles quoted from the Old Testament weren't props; they were light posts to help Israel find its way from Abraham to Jesus.*[2]

Wooden tablets like this one were coated with beeswax to form a writing surface. (Photo Courtesy of the Schoyen Collection, Oslo and London)

Without the Old Testament, it's as if we're trying to start God's storyline in the center, with the inauguration of the kingdom of Christ. That would be like launching your reading of a trilogy by studying the final chapter of the final volume of the book series, or expecting to land in an airplane at your destination without first taking off from your point of departure, or beginning a baseball game at the seventh-inning stretch.

Why the Old Testament Seems So Different

Why, then, does the Old Testament sometimes seem so different from the New?

One reason is simply because the Old Testament is more *distant* and more *diverse* than the New Testament. Do you remember how the author of the letter to the Hebrews described God's revelation in the Old Testament? "Long ago, at many times and in many ways, God spoke" (Hebrews 1:1). This distance ("long ago") and diversity ("many times … many ways") are primary reasons why it can be so difficult to understand the origins of the Old Testament.

Consider a couple of contrasts between the two testaments for a moment:

New Testament	Old Testament
Approximately ten men and their scribes penned the New Testament on parchment and papyrus over the course of a few decades.	The Old Testament developed through a thousand-year process that involved dozens of authors and editors writing in a variety of ways and even God himself etching words in stone.
The New Testament describes less than a century of history under the rule of a single empire.	The Old Testament spans more than 3,000 years of history, encompassing the rise and fall of kingdoms and empires in regions ranging from northern Africa to central Asia.

And yet, even with such a vast distance between these documents and our lives today, there's no reason to despair when it comes to understanding how we got the Old Testament. Anyone, even you, can learn enough about the ancient Hebrew Scriptures to bridge most of these gaps. With that in mind, let's look together at a few of the most significant questions about the beginnings of the Bible:

✢ How did the Old Testament begin?

✦ How was the Old Testament written?

✦ How was the Old Testament preserved?

✦ How were the books in the Old Testament chosen?

What we will learn as we bridge these gaps won't merely multiply our knowledge about a few nomads in the Ancient Near East—it will also strengthen our trust in the reliability of God's Word.

"Long ago, at many times and in many ways, God spoke to our fathers by the prophets, but in these last days he has spoken to us by his Son, whom he appointed the heir of all things, through whom also he created the world."—Hebrews 1:1-2

Testament

(Also, "covenant") A lasting agreement that defines a relationship between two or more parties and requires at least one of them to fulfill specified obligations. God's testaments—or, covenants—with humanity throughout the Bible are like a spine that binds together the entire storyline of Scripture.[3] The holy writings of Israel tell the story of God's covenants with Israel and Israel's failure to keep these covenants. It was the apostle Paul who first referred to these texts as the "old covenant" or "old testament" (2 Corinthians 3:14). These writings looked forward to the "new covenant" or "new testament" that would be fulfilled in Jesus Christ (Jeremiah 31:31-32; Luke 22:20; 1 Corinthians 11:25; 2 Corinthians 3:6; Hebrews 8:1-13; 9:15; 12:24).[4]

How the Bible Began[5]

The first writer of Scripture may well have been God himself.

One of the earliest mentions of written revelation in Scripture was when "the finger of God" etched the Ten Commandments on "tablets of stone" (Exodus 31:18; 32:15–16). Of course, God is a spirit; so, God doesn't possess physical fingers and nails that scratched words into stone! (John 4:24). When Moses wrote that "the finger of God" etched the first edition of the Ten Commandments, he was using human imagery to identify the writer of these commands as God himself.

Unfortunately, Moses threw a temper tantrum shortly afterward and shattered those original stones (which is a bit of a shame since first-edition tablets from the hand of God would have been quite the collector's item). After Moses got a grip on his temper, God issued a second edition of the Ten Commandments (Exodus 34:1). Moses put these tablets in the ark of the covenant (Deuteronomy 10:5)—but then, sometime in the sixth century BC, the Israelites ended up losing track of the ark. Today, as everyone who's watched the *Indiana Jones* films knows, the ark resides in a top-secret United States government warehouse somewhere in Nevada. No, not really. Truth be told, no one knows what happened to the ark or the tablets. Some ancient Jews claimed the prophet Jeremiah hid the ark before the temple was destroyed; others said the ark was lost in Babylon.[6] Either way, no living human knows where those God-carved tablets ended up.

Old Testament

The Old Testament is the first part of the Christian Bible, which tells the story of God's work with the descendants of Abraham and points forward to the New Testament fulfillment of this story in Jesus. The Old Testament was written primarily in Hebrew, with a few portions preserved in a language known as Aramaic. "Testament" translates a Greek word that could also be rendered "covenant" (2 Corinthians 3:14; Hebrews 8:13). Also known as the Hebrew Scriptures, the Jewish Scriptures, or the First Testament.

And so, God himself seems to have been one of the first authors of Scripture. But who was the first human to write Scripture? As far as we know from Scripture, that distinction belongs to Moses. It was Moses who kept records of Israel's early wars, preserved "the words of the Lord," and provided the Israelites with a "Book of the Covenant" (Exodus 17:14; 24:4, 7). Over time, Moses molded the texts that became the first five books of the Bible. Just like Luke who stitched many sources together to compose his Gospel (Luke 1:1–2), Moses most likely drew from a broad range of earlier materials to develop the Torah. Some of these sources originated with Moses, but many materials were probably passed down as oral traditions or fragments of text. Moses even cited one of his sources—"the Book of the Wars of the Lord"—by name (Numbers 21:14–15).

Who Wrote the Old Testament?

In the millennium that followed the life of Moses, other prophets along with priests and kings continued to record revelation "as they were carried along by the Holy Spirit" (2 Peter 1:21). Historical books drew from court records, military reports, personal recollections, and oral traditions (see, for examples, 1 Kings 11:41; 14:19, 29; 15:7, 31; 16:5, 14, 20, 27; 22:45; 2 Kings 8:23; 12:19). King David wrote many of the psalms, and the wisdom of his son Solomon became the source for most of the proverbs and probably for Ecclesiastes and Song of Songs (Song of Solomon) as well. At some point after the Jews were exiled in Babylon, it seems likely that an inspired scribal editor (perhaps Ezra) pulled the texts together, edited them, and arranged them into a collection that was substantially the same as the Old Testament we possess today.[7]

The authors of certain Old Testament books are unknown to us, but this truth doesn't diminish the authority of these texts. The authority of the Old Testament doesn't depend on whether we know details about every human writer. The Old Testament is the divinely inspired history of the people that God chose to prepare the way for Jesus the Messiah. The authority of the Old Testament text is rooted in God's covenant with Israel and in Jesus' recognition that these writings were the inspired revelation of his Father.

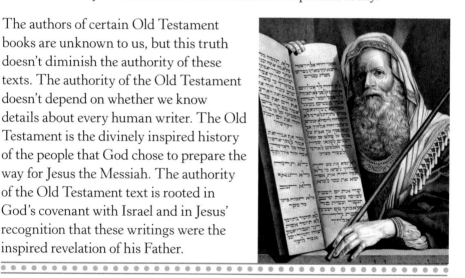

Torah

Hebrew: "instruction, guidance, law." The first five books of the Old Testament, also known as "Pentateuch," from Greek *penta* ("five") and *teuchos* ("containers," "scrolls").[8] The English names for these five books come from the Septuagint, an ancient Greek translation of the Old Testament.

- Genesis (Hebrew *Bereshit*, "In the Beginning")
- Exodus (Hebrew *Shemot*, "Names")
- Leviticus (Hebrew *Vayikra*, "And he called")
- Numbers (Hebrew *Ba Midbar*, "In the Wilderness")
- Deuteronomy (Hebrew *D'Varim*, "Words")

The Writing of the Old Testament — Who and When

Book	Author	Date Written
Genesis, Exodus, Leviticus, Numbers, and Deuteronomy	Moses, with editing and additions by later inspired prophets and scribes	15th century BC, some segments edited or added later
Joshua	Unknown	Unknown, possibly between the 15th and 10th centuries BC
Judges	Unknown	Unknown, perhaps during the reign of David 1010 BC–970 BC
Ruth	Unknown	Unknown, after 11th century BC
1 and 2 Samuel	Unknown	Unknown
1 and 2 Kings	Unknown	Unknown, 6th century BC or later in present form
1 and 2 Chronicles	Unknown	Unknown, probably no earlier than 6th and 5th centuries BC
Ezra	Final author unknown, Ezra 7:27–9:15 (and perhaps more of the book) seems to have been written by Ezra himself	Unknown, after 433 BC
Nehemiah	Unknown, probably same author as Ezra	Unknown, after 433 BC
Esther	Unknown	Unknown, probably after 485 BC
Job	Unknown	Unknown

Book	Author	Date Written
Psalms	Multiple authors: David (73 psalms), Asaph (12 psalms), sons of Korah (11 psalms), Moses (1 psalm), and others. Final editor unknown, possibly Ezra	Individual psalms were produced throughout Israel's history; final form produced sometime after the 6th century BC
Proverbs	Solomon wrote most of the Proverbs. Some proverbs written by "the wise" (22:17–24:22; 24:23–34), Agur (30:1-33), Lemuel (31:1-9), and others	Most proverbs emerged during the reign of Solomon in the 10th century. Eighth-century scribes commissioned by Hezekiah collected and arranged many of Solomon's proverbs (25:1-29:27).
Ecclesiastes	Solomon or someone commissioned by Solomon	10th century BC
Song of Solomon (Song of Songs)	Solomon or someone commissioned by Solomon	10th century BC
Isaiah	Isaiah	Late 8th and early 7th centuries BC, some critical scholars ascribe chapters 40–55 and 56–66 to later writers
Jeremiah	Jeremiah	7th and 6th centuries BC
Lamentations	Jeremiah	6th century BC
Ezekiel	Ezekiel	6th century BC

Book	Author	Date Written
Daniel	Daniel	6th century BC, some critical scholars identify Daniel as fiction and place the writing of the book much later
Hosea	Hosea	Late 8th and early 7th centuries BC
Joel	Joel	Unknown but probably after 586 BC
Amos	Amos	8th century
Obadiah	Obadiah	Unknown, perhaps 6th century
Jonah	Jonah	Unknown, 8th century BC or later
Micah	Micah	Late 8th and early 7th century BC
Nahum	Nahum	7th century BC
Habakkuk	Habakkuk	Unknown, possibly 7th century
Zephaniah	Zephaniah	7th century BC
Haggai	Haggai	520 BC
Zechariah	Zechariah	5th century BC
Malachi	Malachi	5th century BC

How the Old Testament Was Written[9]

But *how* exactly were the words in the Old Testament written?

The stationery stores in ancient Israel didn't sell legal pads or Moleskine® notebooks, after all, and Jeremiah never saw a fountain pen in his life!

That doesn't mean, however, that writing implements were in short supply in the Ancient Near East. The authors of the Old Testament possessed a wide range of surfaces to write on, a couple of different tools to write with, and multiple languages to write in.

What did the writers of the Old Testament write on?

Stone was one of the earliest writing surfaces. Sometimes, words were etched directly into rock (Exodus 34:1). Other times, stones were coated in plaster, and words were painted or impressed in the plaster (Deuteronomy 27:2–3). Clay tablets provided another popular writing surface. Occasionally, texts were etched in copper, silver, or gold (Exodus 28:36).

The most cutting-edge writing surface in the ancient world was the waxed wooden tablet. Wooden panels—about the size of an iPad® — were coated with beeswax. Writers scratched words and sketched ideas in the wax, then they copied the content they wanted to keep on longer-lasting surfaces and scraped the wax surface clean. This may be the process described in Isaiah's prophecies when the prophet is told to "write it before them on a tablet and inscribe it in a book" (Isaiah 30:8). It is possible that some of Isaiah's oracles were scratched on a tablet then preserved on some other surface later. When the beeswax coating wore down to the wood panels, authors recharged their writing devices by re-coating the panels with wax.

A papyrus reed can grow to more than twice the height of an average person and be about as thick as your wrist. Needles were used to separate the pith of the plant into broad, thin strips. These strips were placed in two layers, perpendicular to each other, then pressed together and dried.

Unfortunately, waxed tablets, clay, metal, and stone all share one common problem: any lengthy document written on these surfaces is too large to transport from one place to another. (Glance through the first five books in your Bible; then, imagine trying to carry an entire Torah etched on clay tablets or waxed wood panels. You'd need a pickup truck to transport your Bible every time you headed to church!) That's why the Old Testament books, as they've been passed down to us, were primarily penned on more portable surfaces such as papyrus, leather, and parchment.

Papyrus is a reed that grows in marshy areas (Job 8:11); each plant is about fifteen feet tall and as thick as your wrist. "Paper is made from papyrus," the writings of Roman philosopher Pliny tell us, "by using needlepoints to separate it into thin strips, as wide as possible."[10] These wide strips were stacked in two layers, with one layer laid perpendicular to the other; the layers were pressed together, dried, and rubbed smooth. The Egyptians were writing on papyrus paper more than a thousand years before Moses was born. It seems that Jeremiah's prophecies may have been penned first on papyrus, since these prophecies burned readily when the king pitched them into his fire pot (Jeremiah 36:23).

Another ancient writing surface was leather. Long before Moses led the Israelites out of Egypt, the skins of calves or goats were being soaked in lime, scraped, and tanned to produce a tough but somewhat rough writing material.

It was around the second century BC that leather began to give way to parchment. That's when the king of Egypt started withholding papyrus from Pergamum, a city in western Asia Minor. The Pergamenes didn't despair about their sudden lack of smooth writing surfaces. Instead, they experimented with a process for producing smoother writing surfaces by stretching the animal skins. The smooth and durable product of their experiments became known as "parchment," from the Greek word for a resident of Pergamum.

A few early sources of Old Testament texts may have been etched in tablets of clay, wax, or stone. The documents that the Jewish people preserved as God's inspired Word, however, were copied on papyrus, parchment, and leather. When Paul asked Timothy to bring "the parchments," he may have been asking Timothy to bring his scrolls of the Old Testament (2 Timothy 4:13).

What did the writers of the Old Testament write with?

When etching words in wax, stone, or clay, Old Testament writers used styluses (Job 19:24; Isaiah 8:1; Jeremiah 17:1). When writing on papyrus or leather, the earliest writers used thin-stemmed reeds, frayed on one end to form tiny brushes. Later copyists did their work with stiff reeds, cut at an acute angle to form a point at the end. The most common ink in this era was made by mixing soot with either vegetable oil or the sap of an acacia tree. Scribes tucked ink-filled animal horns and perhaps pen cases into their belts (Ezekiel 9:2–3, 11).

What language did the writers of the Old Testament write in?

Most of the Old Testament was written in Hebrew—a language that can seem very strange to English readers today! One reason why Hebrew seems

strange to us is because it's written right-to-left instead of left-to-right. Also, there's the fact that written Hebrew had no vowels in the Old Testament era—only consonants and a few special characters, known today as "mothers of reading" (*matres lectionis*) to indicate places where vowels should be read. Plus, there were no distinct upper-case and lower-case letters in Hebrew.

Torah scroll containing the book of Exodus. This fourteenth century AD scroll was recovered from a *genizah* (Hebrew, "hiding place") in Cairo where worn-out copies of the Scriptures were discarded. (Photo courtesy of Dunham Bible Museum, Houston Baptist University)

Today, if we tried to write right-to-left with no obvious vowels and no lower-case letters in the English language, one familiar sentence from Scripture would end up looking something like this:

'N' S' DR'L 'HT D'G R'' DR'L 'HT L'RS' ' R'H

Look carefully at the sentence above—remember, read right-to-left not left-to-right—and see if you can decipher these words from Deuteronomy 6:4.[11]

When we consider how the Old Testament was written, it's helpful to know that today's "square-script Hebrew" characters aren't the same letters that the Old Testament authors knew and used. Most of the Old Testament writings would have been written first in "paleo-Hebrew" characters. It wasn't until sometime after the sixth century BC that Jewish scribes began to write Hebrew words using a square-script alphabet that they borrowed from the Assyrians. This alphabet developed into the script that people identify as Hebrew today.

It's also important to know that not all of the Old Testament was written in Hebrew. During their decades of exile, the Jewish people learned Aramaic, a language that was common in ancient commerce and diplomacy. By the time the exile ended, many Jews spoke Aramaic as their first language. (This shift could be why the Levites needed to interpret the Hebrew text that Ezra read to the people, Nehemiah 8:7–8.) It's not surprising, then, that some segments of the Old Testament ended up in Aramaic. A verse in Jeremiah (10:11) as well as two extended sections in Daniel (2:4–7:28) and Ezra (4:8–6:18; 7:12–26) are recorded in Aramaic instead of Hebrew. Since Aramaic used the same square-script alphabet as Hebrew, these texts may look like Hebrew at first glance—but the grammar and vocabulary of Hebrew and Aramaic are as different as English and Latin or Spanish and French! Jews in Judea and Galilee still spoke Aramaic in the first century AD. A handful of Aramaic phrases made their way into the New Testament too, even though the New Testament was written in Greek (Mark 5:41; 7:34; 15:34; Romans 8:15; Galatians 6:4; 1 Corinthians 16:22).

How Hebrew Writing Has Changed

At least as early as the tenth century BC, the Israelites were recording their history and prophecies in paleo-Hebrew. Sometime after the sixth century BC, Jewish scribes shifted to a "square-script" alphabet that can be traced back to the Assyrians.

Square-Script Hebrew

י	ט	ח	ז	ו	ה	ד	ג	ב	א
ר	ק	צ	פ	ע	ס	נ	מ	ל	כ
								ת	ש

Paleo-Hebrew

A dozen fragments among the Dead Sea Scrolls were copied in paleo-Hebrew. The rest of the Hebrew texts among the Dead Sea Scrolls were copied in square script—but, even in the square-script manuscripts, the copyists of the scrolls kept the holy name of God in paleo-Hebrew. Later, the Masoretes—a medieval Jewish scribal sect—added accents, vowel points, and other markings to preserve the correct readings of each biblical text.

Here's how the clause that's translated "Hear, [oh] Israel" (Deuteronomy 6:4) in most English translations looks in each form of Hebrew:

	Paleo-Hebrew
שמע ישראל	Square-script Hebrew
שְׁמַע יִשְׂרָאֵל	Square-script Hebrew with Masoretic vowel points

How the Old Testament Was Preserved

So far, we've learned how the Spirit of God worked through human instruments to inspire the Old Testament Scriptures. But the earliest copies of Scripture—the "autographs"—decayed into dust thousands of years ago! That's partly due to natural processes of deterioration. It's also because foreign nations burned Israel's holy places on multiple occasions and because the Jews disposed of their scrolls whenever they became too worn to use.[13] Every ancient edition of the Old Testament that survives today is a copy. Since these copies come from an era prior to copy machines, computers, and printing presses, all of them were made by hand.

And how accurately did these many generations of not-so-inspired copyists preserve the inspired Scriptures?

Early in the history of Israel, clans of professional copyists emerged to preserve the sacred writings of their people. Some of the descendants of Judah became "clans of scribes" or "Sopherites" (1 Chronicles 2:55). Over time, Jewish copyists developed detailed practices for copying and counting letters to keep every syllable of the text pure.

Near the end of the fifth century AD, a group of Jewish scholars known as the Masoretes (or, Massoretes) standardized and sharpened these ancient practices. Some of the finest surviving manuscripts of the Old Testament come from the Ben Asher family, a Masoretic clan from the region of Tiberias.[14] The Masoretes added vowel markings, accents, and marginal notes to preserve the traditional reading of every text.[15] The Masoretic scribes knew how many words and letters belonged in every book in their Bible. They even knew which word and what letter should stand at the exact center of every book. As a result, the version of the Old Testament preserved by the Masoretes—known today as the Masoretic Text—represents a

Textual Criticism

Textual criticism is the analysis of various copies, fragments, versions, and translations of a text with the goal of recovering the wording of the original manuscript in its final form or forms.[12]

Autograph

The first or original manuscript of a document in its final form is called the *autograph*.

supremely reliable reproduction of the final form of the Old Testament.[16]

Despite the work of the Masoretes and earlier scribal communities, copyists still made mistakes over the centuries. However, when seen in the context of all the manuscripts of the Old Testament, these differences are relatively rare, and none of them affects anything we believe about God's work in the world.[17] When ancient copies differ, the discipline of textual criticism enables scholars to reconstruct the original reading in the overwhelming majority of cases.

The Masoretic Text has always been reliable—but until 1947, no one knew for certain how closely the Masoretic Text followed more ancient texts. The oldest complete copy of the Masoretic Text came from the Middle Ages—more than 1,000 years after the original texts were written!—and the oldest surviving fragment of any Old Testament text was a piece of papyrus from the second century BC.[18] As a result, many skeptics suspected that the Old Testament had changed radically between the time the texts were finalized and the rise of the Masoretes. Then, in 1947, a young shepherd named Muhammed edh-Dhib discovered the Dead Sea Scrolls, and it became clear that the Old Testament had been preserved far more reliably than many skeptical scholars had supposed.

Even before the time of the Masoretes, careful guidelines governed the copying of every Old Testament text. According to the Talmud—a collection of traditions from Jewish rabbis— "every skin must contain a certain number of columns, equal throughout the entire codex. The length of each column must not extend over less than forty-eight or more than sixty lines; and, the breadth must consist of thirty letters; ... An authentic copy must be the exemplar, from which the transcriber ought not in the least deviate; no word or letter ... must be written from memory, the scribe not having looked at the codex before him."[19]

Important Manuscripts from the Masoretes

Manuscript	Date	Description
Codex Leningradensis	Early 11th century AD	Oldest surviving complete manuscript of the Old Testament. The Leningrad Codex was copied by the Ben Asher family of Masoretic scribes.
Aleppo Codex	10th century AD	Masoretic manuscript from Ben Asher. Rioters destroyed Jewish synagogues in the city of Aleppo in 1947, and several portions of this codex were destroyed.
Oriental 4445, British Library Codex of the Pentateuch	10th century AD	Copy of the Torah, attesting to an early form of the Ben Asher Masoretic Text.
Leningrad Codex of the Prophets	10th century AD	Copy of Isaiah, Jeremiah, Ezekiel, and minor prophets, copied from a Ben Asher Masoretic Text.
Codex Cairensis	9th century AD	Ben Asher Masoretic text of the Hebrew prophets.

Aleppo Codex Panel. The marginal markings in the Aleppo Codex are known as "masorah"; these notations provide pronunciations and other information added by Masoretes to preserve the Hebrew and Aramaic text of Scripture.

The Dead Sea Scrolls

Muhammed edh-Dhib had lost his sheep, and he didn't know where to find them.

Or at least that's the story that was told afterward.

Perhaps the sixteen-year-old shepherd was looking for sheep or goats when he tumbled into a desert cave. Or maybe he was looking for ancient tombs that could contain valuable artifacts. According to one local legend, Muhammed tossed a rock into a cave, hoping to find a lost sheep. Yet what he heard when the rock reached its destination wasn't the bleating of a sheep or goat. What he heard instead was the shattering of pottery. What he found in those broken pottery jars would impact the world long after his flock was forgotten.

What Muhammed edh-Dhib found in the winter of 1947 were the first of the Dead Sea Scrolls.

In the decade that followed the initial discovery of seven scrolls, further searches revealed hundreds more fragments and scrolls in ten caves in the region known today as the West Bank. Before it was all over, more than 900 ancient documents were discovered.

Most scholars believe that the Dead Sea Scrolls were the library of a Jewish sect known as the Essenes that had withdrawn to an isolated desert community known as Qumran. This sect formed as a result of controversies related to the Jewish temple in Jerusalem. These disputes prompted the founder of the Qumran sect—known in the scrolls as the "Teacher of Righteousness"—to withdraw from the temple establishment and to establish a community in the desert.

More than 200 of the Dead Sea Scrolls are copies of books in the Hebrew and Aramaic Old Testament. The remaining 700 or so scrolls provide commentaries on the Old Testament as well as rules for living in the Qumran community. These community rules contain some of the more interesting portions of the Dead Sea Scrolls. According to the rules from Qumran, waving at someone with

Old Testament Manuscripts among the Dead Sea Scrolls

Canonical Section (according to the order of the Hebrew and Aramaic text)	Book	Number of Manuscripts*
Pentateuch (*Torah*)	Genesis	24
	Exodus	18
	Leviticus	18
	Numbers	11
	Deuteronomy	33
Prophets (*Neviim*) Former Prophets	Joshua	2
	Judges	3
	1–2 Samuel	4
	1–2 Kings	3
Latter Prophets	Isaiah	22
	Jeremiah	6
	Ezekiel	6
	Twelve (Minor) Prophets	10
Writings (*Ketuvim*) Book of Truth	Psalms	39
	Proverbs	2
	Job	6
Five Small Scrolls	Song of Songs	4
	Ruth	4
	Lamentation	4
	Ecclesiastes	3
	Esther	0
Other books	Daniel	8
	Ezra-Nehemiah	1
	1–2 Chronicles	1
		Total: 232

* There are differing reconstructions of the total number of manuscripts originally represented by the fragmentary texts in the Dead Sea Scrolls; as such, some of these numbers may vary.

your left hand could result in ten days of punishment. Spitting or snorting at something that wasn't supposed to be humorous warranted thirty days of penance. Mooning your neighbor merited a one-month time-out as well.[20]

When the Dead Sea Scrolls were rediscovered in the twentieth century, it became clear that the text of the Old Testament had remained remarkably stable over the centuries. In fact, a scroll of Isaiah found among the Dead Sea Scrolls (1QIsaᵃ) was copied more than a hundred years before Jesus was born; yet, the wording of this scroll of Isaiah agreed almost completely with Masoretic texts that were copied a thousand years later!

In other Old Testament texts, the Dead Sea Scrolls did reveal a wide variety of versions and copying variations that had developed over the centuries—but none of these variants affects anything that we believe about God or about his work in the world. What the Dead Sea Scrolls demonstrated was that, even over the span of centuries, the text of the Old Testament had been copied with exceptional accuracy and care.

The Isaiah Scroll (1QIsa) is the most complete of all the scrolls discovered at Qumran. This scroll includes the entire book of Isaiah and is virtually identical to texts that were copied 1,000 years later than the Dead Sea Scrolls.

Designating the Dead Sea Scrolls

2QSir? 1Q30? 3QPs? Aren't those droids from the *Star Wars* films? Not at all! They're designations for different Dead Sea Scrolls. At first, these designations may seem confusing, but they really aren't complicated at all.

- The *number at the beginning* indicates *in which cave* the document was discovered. 4Q26, for example, was found in the fourth cave.
- The *letter in the middle* indicates the *site* where the document was discovered. Q is an abbreviation for "Qumran."
- The *letters or numbers at the end* indicate either *the content* of the scroll or, if the content isn't obvious, *a number* to distinguish the particular fragment. "Sir" is short for "Sirach," for example, and "Ps" abbreviates "Psalms." A lower-case "p" before the name of a book means that the scroll is a commentary (*pesher*) on that book.

For example, "3QEzek" is a portion of Ezekiel (Ezek) found in the third cave (3) at Qumran (Q), while "1QpHab" is a commentary (p) on Habakkuk (Hab) found in the first cave (1) at Qumran (Q).

Chapter 3

Which Books Belong in the Old Testament?

- The Canon of Scripture
- The Septuagint
- The Apocrypha

Sometimes, you can easily end up in a group where you really don't belong.[1] I learned that lesson a few years ago when I accidentally joined a protest march.

I wasn't in my native nation during my short stint as a protester. I was in Australia, preparing to speak at a conference on theology and family ministry. After flying halfway around the world in less than a day, my body was quite convinced that it was four o'clock in the morning. The sun shining on Sydney, however, insisted it was early afternoon. Concluding that adjusting my internal clock would be simpler than switching the relative positions of the earth and sun, I headed for a walk in Hyde Park.

Paying no attention to where I was going, I meandered into the middle of a crowd around a fountain. When the multitude moved eastward, I moved with them. Suddenly, several dozen homemade placards were thrust into the air and a few participants began to practice a chant.

That's when I realized I had become part of a protest march.

I hadn't planned on becoming a protester when I crossed the Pacific Ocean. I'd meant to talk about ministry and theology—maybe see a kangaroo. But here I was, marching in a crowd of protesters, wondering whether such demonstrations were even legal in Australia. Little by little, I worked my way to the edge of the protest march and finally slipped back into the park. That's how my career as a protester began and ended.

Later that evening, I discovered I'd been protesting the construction of a high-rise building in a nearby neighborhood. I don't know if the Australians ever built that structure in Sydney. I don't even know whether I would have been for it or against it. For the rest of my days down under, I carefully steered clear of all potential protests.

I did learn something important that day in Hyde Park, though: It's easy to become caught up in a group where you really don't belong. And, once you're in that crowd, you can end up identified with a group that's headed somewhere you never intended to go.

That's what seems to have happened with fifteen or so extra texts that appear in some editions of the Old Testament. The Jews never treated these texts— sometimes known as *deuterocanonical* texts or *Apocrypha*—as Scripture. The authors of these documents didn't intend them to be grouped with the books of the Bible, no more than I meant to get caught up in that group of protesters. In fact, the author of one deuterocanonical text specifically pointed out that he lived in a time when prophetic inspiration had ceased.[2] And yet, over the centuries, these texts got caught up in a group of books where they didn't belong; this unintended misgrouping caused them to be identified as divinely-inspired documents when they really weren't inspired at all.

So how did deuterocanonical books end up in some versions of the Old Testament, even though they never belonged there?

It all began in the third and second centuries BC when the Old Testament began to be translated into Greek; these Greek renderings of the Old Testament became known as the *Septuagint*. No one knows precisely why, but the editors of the Septuagint included a range of books that was broader than the Hebrew and Aramaic Scriptures. Nearly 400 years later, Christians began translating the Bible into Latin, and some of them used the Septuagint as their source for translating the Old Testament. In the process, deuterocanonical texts from the Septuagint were translated into Latin alongside the Jewish Scriptures.

When a Christian leader named Jerome developed a new Latin translation of the Old Testament, he used the Hebrew and Aramaic Bible as his primary source, but he translated some deuterocanonical texts from the Greek Septuagint as well. He called these texts "Apocrypha"—meaning "obscure" or "hidden things"—and he made it clear that they should never shape any "doctrines of the church."[4]

Deuterocanonical

From Greek *deutero-* "second" + *kanon* "canon." These are Jewish religious texts included in the Greek Septuagint translation of the Old Testament but not in the Hebrew and Aramaic Old Testament. Also known as "Apocrypha" (from Greek *apokrypha*, "hidden things," "unclear"). Today, Roman Catholic and Orthodox Churches include deuterocanonical texts in their Old Testaments.[3]

Septuagint fragment 4QLXXLev (4Q120) from the Dead Sea Scrolls, 1st century BC.

Another church leader disagreed with Jerome's assessment.

Augustine, the prominent overseer of churches around the North African city of Hippo, believed that the Holy Spirit had superintended not only the original authors of the Old Testament but also the translators of the Septuagint.[5] And so, Augustine took every text and translation in the Septuagint—including the Apocrypha, which the Jews had never treated as Scripture—to be the authoritative Word of God. Three North African church councils concurred with Augustine's opinion—and that is, in part, how the Apocrypha ended up incorporated into the Old Testament. Today, apocryphal writings remain in the Old Testaments of the Orthodox and Roman Catholic Churches.

Vulgate

Latin *vulgo*, "to make common, accessible." The Vulgate is the Latin translation of the Bible by Jerome completed in the fifth century AD.

Septuagint

From Latin *septuaginta*, "seventy." The Septuagint is the Greek version of the Jewish Scriptures, translated in the third century BC and later in Alexandria, Egypt. According to a legend preserved in a forged letter from the second century BC, Demetrius—chief librarian for King Ptolemy II—gathered seventy-two Jewish elders "and invited them to carry out the work of translation. ... They set to work comparing their several results and making them agree, and whatever they agreed upon was suitably copied out. ... It so chanced that the work of translation was completed in seventy-two days. ... When the work was completed, Demetrius collected the Jewish population in the place where the translation had been made, and read it over to all, in the presence of the translators, who met with a great reception from the people." The letter is fanciful but, since more and more Jews were speaking Greek instead of Hebrew or Aramaic, this new translation was well received among Jews throughout the Roman Empire. The number seventy-two was rounded to seventy—*septuaginta* in Latin—and the translation became known as "Septuagint." The Septuagint is frequently abbreviated using the Roman numerals for the number seventy: LXX.

Books of the Apocrypha

✔ = Included in the Bible   ✘ = Not included in the Bible

Book	Description	Status		
		Protestant	Roman Catholic Church	Orthodox Church
1 Esdras	Nearly identical to Ezra in Masoretic Text, with a few additions.	✘	✘	✔
Tobit	While napping beside a courtyard wall, Tobit is blinded by bird droppings. He sends his son with a pet dog to collect a sum of money. A fish tries to eat the son's leg. The son captures the fish and burns its organs on his wedding night to chase away demons that had previously killed his bride's former husbands. The fish's gall heals Tobit's blindness.	✘	✔	✔
Judith	Judith pretends to be a traitor who will provide information so that the Assyrian general Holofernes can conquer her people. She enters his tent while he is drunk and cuts off his head.	✘	✔	✔
Additions to Esther	Additions to the Masoretic Text of Esther.	✘	✔	✔
Wisdom of Solomon	Not written by Solomon; wisdom literature in which many early Christians found prophetic references to Jesus.	✘	✔	✔

Book	Description	Status		
		Protestant	Roman Catholic Church	Orthodox Church
Wisdom of Sirach (Ecclesiasticus)	Wisdom literature, similar to Proverbs.	✗	✔	✔
Baruch	Confession, prayer, and message attributed to Jeremiah's secretary Baruch but written long after Baruch's time	✗	✔	✔
Letter of Jeremiah	Letter attributed to Jeremiah but written long after Jeremiah's time, duplicated in the sixth chapter of Baruch.	✗	✔	✔
Additions to Daniel • Susanna and the Elders • Prayer of Azariah and Song of the Three Young Men • Bel and the Dragon	Daniel, plus the story of a young woman who outwits two elders who try to blackmail her in exchange for sexual favors; a prayer and song added to the story of the fiery furnace; and, a challenge in which Daniel demonstrates that Bel is a false deity.	✗	✔	✔
1 Maccabees	Record of the Jewish rebellion against the Syrians, 175–125 BC.	✗	✔	✔
2 Maccabees	Record of the Jewish rebellion against the Syrians, 180–160 BC.	✗	✔	✔
3 Maccabees	Record of Egyptian persecution of the Jews, 220–200 BC.	✗	✗	✔

How the Canon Was Loaded

Now, all these discussions about misplaced texts and misconstrued contents have probably raised some critical questions in your mind about the Old Testament. Clearly, the Old Testament didn't fall from heaven all at once, bound in leather and edged in gold! But how exactly did the ancient Jews determine which books belonged in the Bible and which ones didn't? And how can we be certain they were correct?

To understand this process, it's important for us first to comprehend the concept of a *canon*.

The Word of God "is living and active," the author of Hebrews declared, "and sharper than any two-edged sword" (Hebrews 4:12). But the Word of God isn't only a sword; it's also a canon. Now, the biblical canon isn't a wheeled weapon that hurls iron balls at your enemies, of course—but "canon" and "cannon" do share the same root.

So what's the common root that ties "canon" and "cannon" together?

It all begins with a reed that grows alongside the Nile River.

The Greek word for this plant was *kanon*. Over the centuries, this word for a tubular reed developed to describe a tubular weapon—a cannon—in English, with the extra "n" picked up from Italian via the Latin *canna*. To envision the link between a riverside reed and a cannon barrel, think about the Italian terms for tubular pasta and pastries, cannelloni and cannoli. (Now, immediately *stop* thinking about cannelloni and cannoli, or you'll end up heading to an Italian restaurant instead of finishing this chapter.)

But how did this word for a tubular reed come to describe the books that are authoritative for God's people?

It started when the Greeks began to cut these reeds—*kanones*—into specific lengths and use them as measuring sticks. A *kanon* became a tool that set standards and measured limits. That's how the word *kanon* came to imply an infallible standard.[6]

In the New Testament, Paul used this term to signify the all-sufficiency of Christ's sacrifice as God's standard—God's *kanon*—for life and faith (Galatians 6:16). By the fourth century AD, the meaning of the word "canon" had expanded to describe the list of writings recognized as the infallible standard for God's people. That's how "canon" came to refer to the Bible, the inerrant record of God's will for his people and his work in the world.[7]

So, how did the ancient Jews identify the books in the Old Testament canon? Did the ancient rabbis parade each book across a stage and give thumbs-up to the texts with the best poise? Or did they drop the prophets into a boxing ring and invite the champions to join the canon? Either of these options would certainly have spiced up our exploration of the canon! The real process was, however, quite a bit calmer and considerably more complex.

How to Recognize What Belongs In the Canon

Evangelical scholars have long recognized that the canon was not created by any human being. The only human role in the making of the canon was recognizing and receiving texts that God had already established. And so, the question isn't, "Who created the canon?" The correct question is, "How and when did God's people recognize the texts that God had already established as authoritative?"

More than a century before Jesus made his first appearance on planet Earth, the Jewish people had already recognized specific authoritative texts that God had established and revealed. These texts are the same ones that appear in the Hebrew and Aramaic Old Testament today. The ancient Jews may never have used the word "canon," but they possessed a clear sense that these texts were uniquely authoritative for their faith and practices.

And how did the Jewish people recognize the texts that God established? Let's look first at the Torah and then at the rest of the Old Testament to find out.

The Torah

Sometimes, the process of receiving a text as God's Word was instantaneous. God himself etched the Ten Commandments in stone (Exodus 31:18; 32:15–16)—a rather unmistakable indication that these words came directly from God! Other texts in the Torah were recognized almost as quickly. God spoke directly with Moses throughout Israel's exodus, and the words that Moses wrote in "the book of the covenant" were immediately received as the words of God (Exodus 24:3–7; 33:11; Numbers 11:10–35). By the time Moses died, the Israelites already possessed a functional canon—a set of authoritative texts that the people recognized as God's Word and that their leaders were called to proclaim and to preserve.

Psalms, Proverbs, and Prophecies

Later, psalms, proverbs, and prophecies built upon God's revelation to Moses. When the proclamations of prophets stood in continuity with God's covenants and their predictions turned out to be true, the people knew that God had inspired these prophets (Deuteronomy 18:21–22). King David commissioned his son to keep every detail of the law of Moses, and his son reflected on these instructions in the books of Proverbs, Ecclesiastes, and Song of Solomon (1 Kings 2:3). Inspired books of history and wisdom reflected further on God's covenant relationships with his chosen people. "As each book of the Old Testament was written, its authority as the revealed Word of God evoked the immediate embracing of it as sacred and binding."[8]

The book of Daniel reveals how quickly this process occurred. In the decades that followed the exile, the prophet Daniel possessed a copy of "the books" or "the Scriptures" (Daniel 9:2)—a settled set of recognized texts—and these texts included not only God's law but also the words of the prophets. Daniel read the writings of the prophet Jeremiah and received his words as the inspired words of God himself (Jeremiah 25:11–12; Daniel 9:2–19).

When God Stopped Speaking

Sometime after their return from exile, the people recognized that prophecies among them had ceased. Three times in the apocryphal books of the Maccabees, the author pointed out that he lived in an era when prophecy had come to an end:

✤ When Judas Maccabeus retook the temple in

164 BC, he and his fellow leaders removed the stones of a defiled altar "until a prophet should appear."

✤ A time of persecution and famine after the death of Judas Maccabeus was identified as "worse than anything that had happened to them since the time when prophets ceased to appear."

✤ The brother of Judas and his descendants were appointed to lead the people "until a true prophet appears."[9]

The Old Testament canon was not created by human guesses or rabbinic councils that happened hundreds of years after the last prophet prophesied. The texts in the Old Testament canon were recognized and received quickly. And, when the time of prophets came to a close, the Jewish people saw that their canon of Scripture was closed as well.

The Covenants That Tie the Old Testament Together[10]

Law	God's covenant with creation (Genesis 1–3; Hosea 6:7) God's covenant with Noah (Genesis 6–9) God's covenant with Abraham (Genesis 15; 17) God's covenant with Israel (Exodus 19–24)
Prophets	God's covenant with David (2 Samuel 7; Psalm 89) God's promise of a new covenant (Jeremiah 31–34; Ezekiel 33–39)
Writings	Reflections on God's continuing covenant faithfulness and love in spite of his people's unfaithfulness

How to Count the Canon

No later than the second century BC, the Jewish people had already identified which texts belonged in their canon, and these texts were arranged in a deliberate order. Although it's impossible to be certain, this deliberate arrangement most likely began around the fifth century BC, in the era of Ezra and Nehemiah.[11] The content in this canon was the same as the content in a Hebrew and Aramaic Old Testament today. Their table of contents, however, looked quite different than the one in your Bible.

If the table of contents in your Bible organizes the books of the Old Testament under different headings, the books are probably clustered into four categories: Law, History, Poetry, and Prophets, perhaps with a distinction between longer prophetic books (Major Prophets) and shorter ones (Minor Prophets).

Not so in the Hebrew Bible!

The Jews living between the Old and New Testaments:

(1) Grouped the books of the Bible in different categories than our Bibles today.[12]

✤ Law: The five books of Moses mingle God's law with history, from the creation of the cosmos to Israel's entrance into the Promised Land.

✤ Prophets: The Prophets join prophecies with historical texts and tell Israel's story from the people's entrance into the Promised Land to their exile from the land.

✤ Writings: The Writings weave wisdom and poetry with scrolls that were read during Israel's festivals and texts that told Israel's history from a different perspective than the Former and Latter Prophets. Since the Psalms are the longest book in the Writings and they stood near the beginning of the Writings, the entirety of this third section of the Jewish Bible was sometimes dubbed "Psalms" or even "David."

(2) Numbered the books in a different way than our Bibles today. If you counted the texts in a Protestant Old Testament, you'd probably come up with a total of thirty-nine books. When Jewish scribes summed the same texts, they counted twenty-four. So how is it possible for the same books to be counted so differently? It's primarily because Jewish scribes copied the prophecies of the twelve shorter prophets—beginning with Hosea and ending with Malachi—on a single scroll and counted them as a single book. Ezra and Nehemiah were originally one book; 1 and 2 Samuel was a single book instead of two, and so were 1 and 2 Kings as well as 1 and 2 Chronicles. Taken together, that accounts for the difference between thirty-nine and twenty-four.

The Canon Jesus Knew

So which arrangement did Jesus and the earliest Christians follow?

One particular passage in Matthew's Gospel makes it clear that the Bible

Jesus knew began with Genesis and ended with Chronicles. Jesus declared that the religious leaders in his day would be held responsible for "all the righteous blood … from the blood of innocent Abel to the blood of Zechariah" (Matthew 23:35).

The death of Abel is the first murder in the Bible, and the murder of Zechariah stands near the end of Chronicles—the last book of the last section in the twenty-four-book Hebrew and Aramaic arrangement of the Old Testament (Genesis 4:8; 2 Chronicles 24:20–22). When Jesus said "from … Abel to … Zechariah," what he meant was "from one end of the canon to the other"—from the beginning of his Bible to the end. Only the three-part Hebrew and Aramaic canon begins with Genesis and ends with Chronicles.

So, if Jesus and the Jewish people in generations before Jesus followed this three-part arrangement, how did the order of the Old Testament end up so jumbled in our English Bibles?

That's because, when the Old Testament was translated into Greek, the editors of the Septuagint rearranged the texts in roughly chronological order and clustered them according to the genre of literature. Latin Bibles followed the Septuagint sequence and so did later English translations.[13] As a result, we possess the same inspired texts that Jesus trusted, arranged in an order that differs from the Bible that Jesus knew—but this difference shouldn't concern us at all. What matters for our faith isn't the *order of* the books but the *testimony in* the books. Our Old Testament texts may not stand in precisely the same sequence as the scrolls that Jesus studied—but our Old Testament contains the same content that his Bible contained. This content is no less trustworthy simply because it is arranged in a different order.

Tanak

From *Torah* + *Neviim* + *Ketuvim*. Tanak is an acronym describing the Jewish Scriptures. The ancient Jews referred to their Hebrew and Aramaic canon as "the Law, the Prophets, and the Writings," "the Law, the Prophets, and the Psalms," "the Law, the Prophets, and David," "the Law, the Prophets, and the other ancestral books"—or simply "the Law and the Prophets" for short. Later, they began to use the word "Tanak" as an even shorter way to refer to their sacred texts. In Hebrew, "Law" comes from the word *Torah*, "Prophets" comes from *Neviim*, and "Writings" from *Ketuvim*. When the first sound is taken from each of these terms, you end up with *Tanak*.

Why Not Have a Loose Canon?

So what about those fifteen or so apocryphal texts that showed up in the Septuagint? What are we missing by excluding these documents from our daily devotional readings? Why not loosen the canon and include them in our Old Testaments?

For the most part, the teachings in the Apocrypha agree with the message that's embedded in the Old and New Testaments—though there are a few contradictions.[14] It's even possible that the author of Hebrews was alluding to a passage in the Apocrypha when he wrote, "Some men were tortured, not accepting release, so that they might gain a better resurrection" (Hebrews 11:35).[15] And the apocryphal texts *do* provide a valuable historical perspective on the era between the final Old Testament prophets and the births of John the Baptist and Jesus the Messiah. That's why sixteenth-century pastor and reformer Martin Luther wrote regarding these texts: "These are books that, though not esteemed like the holy Scriptures, are still both useful and good to read."[16]

So, if the apocryphal texts are "useful and good to read," why not include them in the canon?

When considering whether a text belongs in the canon of Scripture, what matters most is not the *usefulness* of the text but the *source* and the *purpose*.

> When considering whether a text belongs in the canon of Scripture, what matters most is not the *usefulness* of the text but the *source* and the *purpose*.

Remember: the canon is not a human creation; the canon was formed by recognizing and receiving texts that God had already inspired. Unnumbered multitudes of writings throughout the ages have been useful, and many of them have even told the truth—but the only ones that belong in the canon are those that God himself inspired "for teaching, for rebuking, for correcting, for training in righteousness" (2 Timothy 3:16–17).

So, did the authors of the Apocrypha write words "from God as they were moved by the Holy Spirit"? (2 Peter 1:21). Or were their words merely their "own interpretation" of God's workings in the world? (2 Peter 1:20).

A long line of Christians throughout history have concluded that the apocryphal writings were not God-breathed for three simple reasons:

1. The authors of the New Testament never quoted the Apocrypha as Scripture. The New Testament writers frequently used phrases like "it is written" or "Scripture says" when quoting Old Testament Scripture (for examples, see John 19:37; Romans 3:10; 1 Peter 2:6; Hebrews 3:7). Yet no New Testament author ever applied any of these clauses to any apocryphal text. When quoting the Old Testament, the New Testament authors seem to have cited the Greek Septuagint about two-thirds of the time, yet they never quoted any of the Apocrypha as Scripture—even though the Septuagint included the Apocrypha! Not even one of the few possible New Testament allusions to the Apocrypha is a quotation; each of these allusions is, at best, a vague hint. New Testament authors *did* sometimes draw from Jewish pseudepigraphal texts, and they may have alluded to the Apocrypha from time to time—but they never treated these texts as authoritative, and they never gave the slightest indication that any of them should be counted among the Scriptures.[17]

Pseudepigrapha

From Greek *pseudes* "false" + *epigraphe* "ascription." In a general sense, pseudepigrapha refers to any text attributed in the text itself to someone who was not actually the author of that text. In biblical studies, these are falsely-ascribed Jewish or Christian texts that were never considered canonical by any Jewish or Christian sect.[18]

2. The Jewish people never recognized the Apocrypha as Scripture. According to Jewish historian Josephus, the Jews did not consider these later writings "of equal value" with Scripture because of "the failure of the exact succession of the prophets."[19] Even in the first and second centuries AD, Jews like Josephus knew that the time of inspired prophecy had ended with the Hebrew and Aramaic texts in the Law, Prophets, and Writings.

3. Jesus recognized the three-part Hebrew and Aramaic canon as Scripture. The Scriptures that Jesus recognized were segmented into Law, Prophets, and other writings (Luke 24:44)—and only the Hebrew and Aramaic canon is arranged into these three segments. The Scriptures that Jesus recognized also began with Genesis and closed with Chronicles (Matthew 23:35)—and only the Hebrew and Aramaic canon ends with Chronicles. What these facts reveal is that the text Jesus received as the revelation of his Father's work with Israel did not include the Apocrypha. Jesus recognized and revered the three-part Hebrew and Aramaic canon— which never included the Apocrypha.

This last point is most crucial. As Christians, we take our canonical cues from Jesus and his apostles. They followed the perspective of their fellow Jews and recognized a three-part Hebrew and Aramaic Old Testament that included the same texts as our thirty-nine-book Old Testament today. Jesus himself confirmed this canon; as his followers, so should we.

Like a certain conference speaker who ended up in the wrong crowd and accidentally protested a high-rise building, the Apocrypha may be helpful and well-intended but, when these texts are included in the canon, they're in the wrong crowd.

Where Is the Canon Aimed?

The canon of the Old Testament is crucial—but this canon was never intended to tell the whole story. God's covenants with Noah and Abraham, Israel and David, constituted the first act in a narrative that is larger than the cosmos and longer than time. From the very beginning, the Old Testament canon was aimed toward a greater goal, and that greater goal was the kingdom of God in Christ. All three sections of the Hebrew and Aramaic canon find their fulfillment in the risen Lord Jesus Christ (Luke 24:44). And so, four centuries after the final prophecy in the Old Testament canon was uttered, an angelic messenger was sent to earth, and new words from the Spirit of God began to be spoken again among the people of God (Luke 1:5–80).

The 24 Books of the Old Testament Canon[20]

Probable original arrangement in 24 books	Later traditional arrangement in 24 books
Law (*Torah*) 1. Genesis 2. Exodus 3. Leviticus 4. Numbers 5. Deuteronomy Prophets (*Neviim*) Former Prophets 6. Joshua 7. Judges 8. Samuel (1 and 2 Samuel) 9. Kings (1 and 2 Kings) Latter Prophets 10. Jeremiah 11. Ezekiel 12. Isaiah 13. Book of the Twelve (Hosea, Joel, Amos, Obadiah, Jonah, Micah, Nahum, Habakkuk, Zephaniah, Haggai, Zechariah, Malachi) Writings (*Ketuvim*) 14. Ruth 15. Psalms 16. Job 17. Proverbs 18. Ecclesiastes 19. Song of Solomon 20. Lamentations 21. Daniel 22. Esther 23. Ezra-Nehemiah 24. Chronicles (1 and 2 Chronicles)	Law (*Torah*) 1. Genesis 2. Exodus 3. Leviticus 4. Numbers 5. Deuteronomy Prophets (*Neviim*) Former Prophets 6. Joshua 7. Judges 8. Samuel (1 and 2 Samuel) 9. Kings (1 and 2 Kings) Latter Prophets 10. Isaiah 11. Jeremiah 12. Ezekiel 13. Book of the Twelve (Hosea, Joel, Amos, Obadiah, Jonah, Micah, Nahum, Habakkuk, Zephaniah, Haggai, Zechariah, Malachi) Writings (*Ketuvim*) Book of Truth 14. Psalms 15. Proverbs 16. Job Five Small Scrolls (*Megilloth*) 17. Song of Solomon 18. Ruth 19. Lamentations 20. Ecclesiastes 21. Esther Other Writings 22. Daniel 23. Ezra-Nehemiah 24. Chronicles (1 and 2 Chronicles)

How We Got the
New Testament

Have you ever been tempted to let a whining child watch a questionable movie or read a popular book without familiarizing yourself with it first?

The next time you're tempted to give in to the demands of a petulant preteen, remember the story of a man named Serapion.

It was late in the second century AD when Serapion took the position of overseer in the church at Antioch. As the leading pastor in Antioch, Serapion was responsible not only for the churches in his own city but also for congregations scattered throughout Syria. Soon after Serapion became pastor at Antioch, troubling news reached him from the nearby village of Rhossus.

The church in Rhossus was in an uproar. When Serapion paid a pastoral visit to Rhossus, he found church members arguing over whether they ought to read a retelling of the life of Jesus that had been presented to them "under Peter's name." Serapion had never studied this book for himself. Still, he did what every parent has been tempted to do at some point when faced with squabbling children: hoping to quiet the combatants, he gave in to their demands.

"If this is the only thing that seems to produce meanness of soul among you," Serapion said, "let it be read."[1] Put in more contemporary terms, the pastor's point ran something like this: "You all are arguing with each other over this little book? If that's your only problem, go ahead and read it."

It's unclear whether the residents of Rhossus wanted to study the so-called Gospel of Peter as Scripture or if a few folk simply hoped to include this text in their devotional readings.[2] Either way, it wasn't long before Serapion regretted what he'd permitted!

Trusted sources informed Serapion that the church members who were pushing Gospel of Peter had a defective perspective on the humanity of Jesus. Then, a copy of Gospel of Peter finally made its way from Rhossus to Antioch. When Serapion studied the text for himself, he found "the greater part to be in accordance with the Savior's right word—but with certain things expanded." These expansions were so serious that they triggered a reversal of Serapion's earlier approval.[3]

What Did Serapion Discover?

Most of the exaggerations that Serapion read were strange but not heretical. According to *Gospel of Peter*, Jesus seemed to tower taller than the sky when he erupted from the tomb. After the resurrection, a voice thundered from the heavens, "Have you proclaimed to those that are asleep?" and a towering cross replied, "Yes."[4]

Other portions in *Gospel of Peter* were, however, more problematic than a sky-high Savior and a talking cross. Christ on the cross was—according to *Gospel of Peter*—"quiet, as one having no pain."[5] Some second-century church members seem to have taken texts like this to mean that Jesus Christ was a supra-human spirit, not truly human at all. That's part of what tipped off Serapion to the fact that this so-called "Gospel" hadn't come from the apostle Peter—and that's why Serapion dashed off a breathless letter to the church in Rhossus as soon as he finished studying *Gospel of Peter*.

"We accept [the writings of] Peter and the other apostles just as [we would accept] Christ," Serapion wrote, "but, as for those with a name falsely ascribed, we deliberately dismiss them, knowing that no such things have been handed down to us. ... I will hurry to be with you again; expect to see me shortly."[6]

Not long after a messenger delivered this letter to the church in Rhossus, Serapion rushed out his front door and headed northwest on the rocky coastal road that led to Rhossus, hoping to stop the spread of the so-called *Gospel of Peter*.

How Did Early Christians Determine Which Texts Were True?

So what lessons can we learn from this second-century church squabble?

First off, it's probably a good idea to read a book for yourself before you encourage someone else to read it!

More important for the purposes of this study, we see that early Christians didn't spend centuries wringing their hands, wondering what sorts of writings they ought to receive as God's Word. Sure, there were decades of conversations and controversies regarding a tiny handful of texts. Yet, even in the earliest decades of church history, Christians received writings that could be traced to apostolic eyewitnesses as the authoritative words and will of Jesus Christ. From the very beginning, Christians received the testimonies of the apostles and eyewitnesses of Jesus as authoritative, and they took the New Testament Gospels to be reliable records of the life and work of Jesus. Writings like *Gospel of Peter* that came later or contradicted the eyewitness accounts could not be considered authoritative.

Did Early Christians Care Who Wrote Their Scriptures?

What's more, early Christians cared deeply about whether their texts were written by the people whose names were ascribed to them. According to Serapion, churches in his region rejected writings with an author's "name falsely ascribed." If the authenticity of a text was in question, early Christians appraised the truthfulness of the text by comparing the content with the "Savior's right word" in the writings "handed down to us"—most likely, a reference to undisputed apostolic writings such as the four Gospels and Paul's letters to the churches.

But how exactly were the earliest testimonies about Jesus preserved and written? Were there other writings that some Christians considered authoritative? Were there "lost Gospels," and, if so, are they still lost today?

To find the answers to these questions and more, let's trace the development of the New Testament from the Spirit of God through the hands of people and into the text that we treasure still today.

Can We Trust the
New Testament?

The witch's knife plunged deep into the lion's heart, and the majestic creature quivered and died. For a few seconds, complete silence descended on the movie theater. A slight sniffling beside me broke the stillness, and that's when I heard my nine-year-old daughter whisper a rather profound word of wisdom to her friend.

A few months earlier, my daughter Hannah had heard that the book *The Lion, the Witch, and the Wardrobe* was being adapted into a feature film. I made it clear to her that she wouldn't be allowed to see the movie until she first read the fantasy novel by C. S. Lewis. Then, I added a challenge: If she would read all seven books in the series before the movie was released, I would take her and her friend Lacey to see the movie on opening day. Three weeks later, Hannah had devoured all of the *Chronicles of Narnia*; so, on the afternoon of the film's release, I found myself in a packed theater with two girls, watching *The Lion, the Witch, and the Wardrobe*.

Since Hannah had already read the book, the storyline of the film was familiar to her—but her friend hadn't yet read *The Lion, the Witch, and the Wardrobe*. For Lacey, the tale of the lion who returns from the dead after giving his life to save a traitor was all new. Still, when the witch's knife fell and Aslan the lion died, both children were moved to tears. The difference was that Hannah knew what happened next. It was in that moment that I heard Hannah lean over and whisper these words of comfort to her friend: "Don't worry; I read the book. He doesn't stay dead."

That's what we as Christians believe as we read the New Testament.

For nearly 2,000 years, Christians have confessed together that, because the one who died on Good Friday didn't stay dead, our despair can never speak the final word. But, unlike the resurrection of Aslan the lion, the resurrection of Jesus Christ was no storybook fantasy! The resurrection of Christ happened in history, and Christ himself has promised that everyone who trusts in him will share in his new life. And so, we as Christians declare with confidence, "Don't worry; I read the book. He didn't stay dead."

Reliable Testimony or Telephone Game Gone Bad?

But how certain can we be that the story of Jesus and his resurrection really happened in history? What if the authors of the New Testament never intended their words to be taken as reliable reports about the life of Jesus in the first place? What if their writings contained far more fantasy than history?

Those are precisely the possibilities that certain skeptical scholars have popularized over the past few decades. The New Testament Gospels were—according to one such scholar—

> written thirty-five to sixty-five years after Jesus' death, not by people who were eyewitnesses, but by people living later. ... After the days of Jesus, people started telling stories about him in order to convert others to the faith. ... Stories were changed with what would strike us today as reckless abandon. They were modified, amplified, and embellished. And sometimes they were made up.[1]

Another scholar of religions claims that "The gospels are not, nor were they ever meant to be, a historical documentation of Jesus's life."[2]

One of these scholars even compares the spread of the stories about Jesus to "Telephone"—the children's game where one person in a circle whispers a sentence to someone else, and that person whispers what she or he hears to the next person, and so on, all the way around. At the end, the first person and the last person reveal their sentences, and everyone laughs at how much the sentence changed between the first and final communicators. Here's how this particular skeptic depicts the development of the stories about Jesus:

> Imagine playing "Telephone" ... over the expanse of the Roman Empire (some 2,500 miles across!) with thousands of participants from different backgrounds, with different concerns, and in different contexts. ... Stories based on eyewitness accounts are not necessarily reliable, and the same is true a hundredfold for accounts that—even if stemming from reports of eyewitnesses—have been in oral circulation long after the fact.[3]

Now, it's true that several years stand between the life of Jesus and the first surviving texts written about him. Paul's letters to the Galatians and the Thessalonians are some of the earliest writings in the New Testament, after all, and these letters were penned around AD 50. What that means is that two decades stand between the time when Paul wrote his first letters and the days when Jesus walked and talked with his disciples.[4] The New Testament Gospels were written even later than Paul's letters, sometime between AD 60 and AD 100.

Nevertheless, when I look at the New Testament texts in their cultural contexts, I find that skeptical suppositions about these texts quickly fall apart. In fact, each time I study the origins of the New Testament, I find myself more and more convinced that the traditions in the New Testament are traceable to reliable testimonies from trustworthy witnesses—not to an ancient game of Telephone gone bad.

How Early Christians Kept Testimonies about Jesus True to Their Sources

Suppose that you need to remember a list of items today.

How will you make certain you don't forget any of the items on your list?

If you're like me, you'll use a fountain pen to inscribe each item in a Moleskine® journal; others might grab a ball-point pen and scrawl their list on the palm of their hand. If you're more technologically inclined, you may tap your to-do list into your smartphone. The precise tools may change, but the pattern remains the same: In contemporary Western culture, if we need to remember something, we write it down. Throughout the past half-millennium, civilizations with their roots in Europe have developed a deep reliance on reading and writing to remember.

Today, this reliance on writing has merged with new technologies so that stories leap almost instantly from eyewitness testimonies to written words. Moments after an event occurs, firsthand reports and secondhand speculations are already trending on social media. By the next morning, the story has flooded the front pages of every newspaper and news website. Within a few weeks, mass-printed books about the event are crawling up the *New York Times* Best Sellers list.

If you've spent your entire life in a culture like this—where information races rapidly from personal experiences to written reports—it's easy to assume that stories can't circulate reliably for very long unless they're written down. That's why some Christians become concerned about the reliability of the Gospels when skeptics point out that these books were written decades after Jesus' death.

The problem with the skeptics' claims is that they're trying to force an ancient culture to fit into the mold of modern expectations. Unlike most of us, the earliest Christians didn't live in a culture of widespread writing and literacy. They lived in an *oral culture*. In ancient oral cultures, experiences didn't need to be written immediately in a literary form. People in these contexts were capable of sharing oral testimonies reliably over the course of decades without ever writing them down. Criticizing testimonies in ancient oral cultures because they weren't written down as quickly as we would write them today is like criticizing George Washington because he never flew in an airplane! It's expecting people from long ago in another culture to follow patterns that didn't emerge until hundreds of years later.

So why did people in the first century AD rely so heavily on oral testimonies?

Oral Culture

A culture in which stories and memories are recalled and shared primarily through spoken words instead of written words.

Reliance on oral testimonies in the first century was partly due to widespread illiteracy. Fewer than half the people in the Roman Empire could read; fewer still were able to write.[5] Oral histories—spoken testimonies to truth, memorized and shared in communities during the lifetimes of the eyewitnesses—were far more fruitful forms of information for people who couldn't read or write.[6]

And what kept these oral histories from degenerating into an empire-wide game of Telephone?[7]

(1) People in oral cultures were capable of recalling and repeating oral histories accurately. In the oral culture of the first Christians, many people were trained from childhood to memorize entire libraries of laws and stories, poetry and songs.[8] Rhythmic patterns and mnemonic devices were woven into oral histories so that learners could quickly convert spoken testimonies into permanent memories.[9] God worked through this cultural pattern to preserve the truths that we read today in the New Testament. That's why a gap between spoken reports and written records wasn't a significant cause for concern among the first Christians.

(2) Christian communities worked together to keep oral histories true to their sources. Oral histories weren't preserved by isolated individuals; they were preserved in communities. This was especially true when it came to early testimonies about Jesus. To be a Christian in the first century was to live enmeshed in a congregation of fellow believers. The stories of Jesus were memorized and shared in the context of a tight-knit fellowship of faith. If one member's retelling of a story misconstrued the original testimony, other members of the community could quickly correct the error.[10]

(3) Eyewitnesses kept testimonies connected to the original events. Early Christian communities weren't the only checks that kept testimonies about Jesus tied to historical truth. Throughout the decades that separated the earthly ministry of Jesus from the writing of the New Testament, living eyewitnesses of the risen Lord Jesus were still circulating in the churches.[11] If embellished testimonies had started to multiply among early Christians, eyewitnesses could curtail the falsehoods and restate the truth about the events.[12]

Did the Testimonies that Became Part of the New Testament Change Over Time?

So were the oral histories about Jesus "modified, amplified, and embellished" over the years, as skeptical scholars claim?

Not even close.

In fact, evidences from the first century AD show that testimonies about Jesus remained remarkably stable as they spread across the Roman Empire.

Let's take a look at one of Paul's letters to see clear evidence for the reliability of the oral histories. When Paul included one of these testimonies in a letter to the Corinthians, he prefaced the testimony by saying, "I would remind you ... of the gospel I preached to you. ... For I delivered to you as of first importance what I also received" (1 Corinthians 15:1–3, ESV).[13] In other words, "I'm about to say again what I said when I was with you—and, remember, what I said to you back then wasn't anything I made up! It was what I received from people who knew the facts firsthand." Paul then proceeded to recite the testimony he had previously shared with them:

> *"That Christ died for our sins in accordance with the Scriptures,*
>
> *"that he was buried,*
>
> *"that he was raised on the third day in accordance with the Scriptures, and*
>
> *"that he appeared to Cephas, then to the twelve.*
>
> *"Then he appeared to more than five hundred brothers at one time. ...*
>
> *"Then he appeared to James, then to all the apostles"*
> *(1 Corinthians 15:4–7, ESV).*

So when did Paul first learn this oral history? Most likely, from Simon Peter, soon after Paul trusted Jesus (Galatians 1:18).

And when had Paul taught this testimony to the Corinthians? That happened four or five years before he recorded these words in his first letter to the Corinthian church. Paul's proclamation of the gospel in Corinth happened in the year 50, and he wrote 1 Corinthians from the city of Ephesus around AD 54 (Acts 18:1–19:22; 1 Corinthians 16:8, 19).

Now, let's consider carefully what this text reveals about oral histories in the first century: Paul recorded the testimony

The apostle Paul wrote his first surviving letters in AD 49 and 50. Paul continued to write letters to the churches until his death around AD 65.

in a letter to the Corinthians at least four years after he first taught them this oral history. If Paul had altered this testimony between the time he first taught the Corinthians and the moment he wrote his letter, the members of the Corinthian church would have noticed the changes. But Paul hadn't modified his message in the least! The testimony he recorded in his first letter to the Corinthians was identical to the testimony he had taught them years before—and it was the same message that Paul repeated in city after city as he crisscrossed the Roman Empire.

And so, is it true—as skeptics have claimed—that teachings and testimonies about Jesus "were changed with what would strike us today as reckless abandon"?[14] Not as far as we can tell from the testimony in Paul's letter to the Corinthians. When Paul dictated the testimony that's recorded in 1 Corinthians 15:3–7, he repeated words that were identical to the ones he had taught the Corinthians years earlier. There is no reason to think that other testimonies that made their way into the New Testament circulated any less reliably than this one.

Yes, two decades stand between the cross of Jesus and the earliest surviving records about Jesus—but that doesn't mean that testimonies about Jesus were somehow mangled beyond recovery. There is clear evidence in Paul's letter to the Corinthians that the authors of the New Testament repeated and wrote the same testimonies they received. When they composed letters and Gospels, these authors drew from a rich range of oral testimonies and teachings from people who had seen the risen Lord.[15] Sometimes, they recited exact testimonies that their readers already knew (1 Corinthians 11:23–25; 15:3–7). Other times, they applied Jesus's teachings without quoting them word-for-word (Romans 14:14; 1 Corinthians 7:10–11; 9:14)—but there's no substantive proof that the authors of the New Testament fabricated the words and works of Jesus.

Apostle

From Greek *apostolos*, "sent out," "commissioned." A witness of the resurrection of Jesus Christ (Acts 1:22) and recipient of his teachings (Ephesians 3:5), commissioned to safeguard the gospel and to apply the teachings of Jesus in the churches. Occasionally applied more broadly to individuals sent on a mission (Acts 14:4, 14).

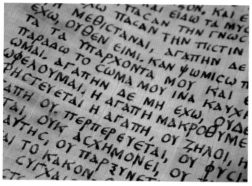

1 Corinthians 13 in Koine Greek

Greek

The New Testament was written in the *Koine* ("common") dialect of the Greek language. In the centuries leading up to the birth of Jesus, *Koine* Greek was the common language spoken throughout the Roman Empire.

How the Epistles Were Written

It was in the mid-first century that the earliest writings about Jesus Christ started to circulate in the churches. The authors of these early epistles were apostles—Christ-commissioned eyewitnesses of the resurrection. The purpose of their writings wasn't to provide information about Jesus. Their goal was to apply the message of Jesus in the lives of people who already knew about Jesus, and their words carried the same authority in the churches as Jesus himself (1 Corinthians 14:37).

If you write an email today, you'll probably compose and send the email without anyone else's help. That's because you're completely capable of typing the words yourself, and the World Wide Web will take care of delivering your electronic epistle. It wasn't that way with the letters that survive in the New Testament today! It took a team of trustworthy men and women to convey each of these letters from the mind of an apostolic witness to the gathered people of God.

Epistle

From Greek, *epistole*, meaning "letter." Written correspondence intended to be read publicly.

In the first place, it's unlikely that Peter or James or Paul ever sat down with a pen in hand to write a letter in his own handwriting. Instead, the apostles spoke God-inspired truth to secretaries who shaped the content into written letters.[16] Each letter was then reviewed and—in some cases—signed by the author (2 Thessalonians 3:17; see also 1 Corinthians 16:21; Galatians 6:11; Colossians 4:18). Most of these secretaries have remained anonymous over the centuries. A couple of them are, however, mentioned by name in the apostles' letters. Tertius composed

Paul's letter to the Romans, for example, while Silvanus probably crafted Simon Peter's first letter (Romans 16:22; 1 Peter 5:12).[17]

Secretaries like Tertius and Silvanus used reed pens, sharpened and slit at the tips. The tips of the reeds were dipped in a mixture of water, soot, and sap; words were then inked on sheets of papyrus. If the letter was lengthy, papyrus sheets were pasted together to form scrolls that might measure as many as thirty or thirty-five feet when unrolled.[18] Once a letter was finished, a trustworthy messenger carried the scroll to a local church and probably read the contents in a public assembly.[19] Messengers mentioned by name in the New Testament include Phoebe, Epaphroditus, and Tychicus (Romans 16:1–2; Ephesians 6:21–22; Philippians 2:25; Colossians 4:7–9). Once a letter reached a church, it might be copied and shared with other churches (Colossians 4:16). That's how first-century churches began to gather and to preserve the epistles that we find in the New Testament today.

What Happened to the Autographs?

The original manuscripts of the Bible in their final form are known as the *autographs*. The autographs of the New Testament decayed into dust many centuries ago—but there is some evidence that the autographs might have survived at least until the end of the second century. Around AD 180, Tertullian of Carthage wrote, "You who are ready to exercise your curiosity, ... run over to the apostolic churches ... where their own authentic writings are read."[20] "Authentic writings" may refer to the original documents sent by apostles—especially since Tertullian follows this statement by listing the specific cities where the first-century apostles sent their epistles.

Books of the New Testament

Book	Sender	Date	Background
James	James, Jesus' half brother	Mid 1st century, perhaps later	Perhaps written to Jewish Christians outside of Palestine.
Galatians	Paul	48/49	Written to churches of South Galatia that Paul visited on his first missionary journey.
1 Thessalonians	Paul, Silvanus (Silas), and Timothy	50	Written to the churches of Thessalonica. Written during Paul's second missionary journey from the city of Corinth.
2 Thessalonians	Paul, Silvanus (Silas), and Timothy	50	Written to the churches of Thessalonica soon after the first letter.
1 Corinthians	Paul and Sosthenes	53 or 54	Written from Ephesus to the church of Corinth.
2 Corinthians	Paul and Timothy	54 or 55	Most likely written from Macedonia, perhaps from Phillipi.
Romans	Paul; Tertius served as Paul's secretary	Mid- to late 50s	Perhaps written during Paul's stay in Greece.
Philippians	Paul	Late 50s	Written during Paul's imprisonment in Rome.
Ephesians	Paul	Early 60s	Written during Paul's imprisonment in Rome. May have been a letter intended for several churches including the church in Laodicea (see Colossians 4:16).
Colossians	Paul	Early 60s	Written during Paul's imprisonment in Rome.

Book	Sender	Date	Background
Philemon	Paul	Early 60s	Written during Paul's imprisonment in Rome.
Mark	John Mark, Simon Peter's interpreter	Mid-60s	Probably written in Rome.
Matthew	Matthew	Late 60s or later in Greek, perhaps earlier in Aramaic	Written for a Jewish audience.
Titus	Paul	Early to mid-60s	Written to Titus who was in Crete when the letter was written.
1 Timothy	Paul	Early to mid-60s	Written in Macedonia to Timothy, who was in Ephesus at the time.
2 Timothy	Paul	Early to mid-60s	Likely written during Paul's second imprisonment in Rome to Timothy, who was possibly in Rome as well.
1 Peter	Peter Silvanus may have served as Peter's secretary	Early 60s	Peter said that he was writing from "Babylon" (5:13); this was probably a metaphor for Rome.
2 Peter	Peter	Mid-60s	Probably written near the end of Peter's life.
Hebrews	Unknown	Unknown	Unknown authorship, received as apostolic due to the connection with the apostle Paul's protégé Timothy (Hebrews 13:23).
Luke	Luke	Late 60s or later	Written to Theophilus, perhaps Luke's literary patron.

Book	Sender	Date	Background
Acts	Luke	Late 60s or later	Written to Theophilus, perhaps Luke's literary patron.
John and 1 John	John the apostle	Late 1st century	Probably written from Ephesus.
2 and 3 John	John, perhaps the apostle or perhaps another eyewitness from the apostolic era known as "John the elder"	Late 1st century	Perhaps written from Ephesus.
Revelation	John, probably the apostle	Late 60s during the reign of Emperor Nero, or 90s during the reign of Emperor Domitian	Written on the island of Patmos to churches in Ephesus, Smyrna, Pergamum, Thyatira, Sardis, Philadelphia, and Laodicea.

How the Gospels and Acts Were Written

But what happened once the apostles and eyewitnesses began to pass away? How were the testimonies about Jesus preserved? And what kept these testimonies from degenerating into myths and legends?

The answer is found in the four New Testament Gospels.

All four of the New Testament Gospels were written in the lifetimes of the eyewitnesses, and their testimony can be traced back to firsthand encounters with Jesus himself.[21] Here's a report from a second-century Christian named Irenaeus of Lyon about the origins of each Gospel:

> Matthew published his Gospel among the Hebrews in their own language while Peter and Paul were preaching and founding the

church in Rome. After their departure, Mark—the disciple and translator of Peter—passed down to us in writing those things that Peter preached. Luke—the attendant of Paul—recorded in a book the Gospel that Paul declared. Afterward, John—the disciple of the Lord, who leaned against the Lord's side—published his Gospel while living at Ephesus in Asia.[22]

If Irenaeus rightly recalled the origins of the Gospels, the apostle Matthew wrote his Gospel while Peter and Paul were in Rome. Paul preached the gospel in Rome while under house arrest in the early 60s AD (Acts 28:11–31); that would mean Matthew's Gospel was written thirty years or so after the first reports of Jesus' resurrection. A few years after Paul preached in Rome, Emperor Nero claimed that Christians had started a fire that scorched much of Rome. In the persecution that followed, Peter and Paul were executed for their faith. The Gospel According to Mark, which was based on eyewitness testimony from the apostle Peter, was published soon after the martyrdoms of Peter and Paul ("their departure," in the words of Irenaeus). That lands Mark's Gospel in the mid-60s AD.

Irenaeus of Lyon learned from Polycarp of Smyrna who personally knew eyewitnesses of the risen Lord Jesus.

There's a bit of a riddle here when it comes to the origins of Matthew's Gospel. According to church leaders like Irenaeus, the Gospel According to Matthew was composed in the language of the Hebrew people—Aramaic, most likely—prior to the writing of Mark's Gospel. Yet the version of Matthew's Gospel that survives today is written in Greek and incorporates most of Mark's Gospel! This fact raises a couple of important questions about the origins of Matthew's Gospel: What happened to the Aramaic version of Matthew? And how did so much of Mark's Gospel end up in Matthew's Gospel? One possibility is that the Gospel According to Matthew was issued in two editions—an Aramaic version that's been lost and a Greek version that merged Mark's Gospel with a Greek edition of Matthew's Gospel.[23]

Luke the Gospel-writer never encountered Jesus in the flesh—but, as Paul's traveling companion, he knew people who had personally seen and heard Jesus.[24] Sometime in the second half of the first century, Luke crafted a Gospel from the testimonies of these "eyewitnesses and servants of the word" (Luke 1:1–3). Much like Matthew, Luke seems to have used Mark's Gospel as a framework for his narrative. Unlike Matthew and Mark, Luke didn't stop his story with the post-resurrection appearances of Jesus. Luke's Gospel was the first volume in a two-part history that he continued in the Acts of the Apostles.[25]

The author of the fourth Gospel was one of the last living eyewitnesses of the life of Jesus. John had leaned against Jesus' side; he had watched his Savior die; and, he had eaten breakfast on the lakeshore beside the risen Lord (John 13:23; 19:35; 21:24). In the closing decades of the first century, John recorded his recollections of the life of Jesus in a Gospel. Just as the apostles Peter and Paul worked with secretaries to write their letters, it's entirely likely that Gospel-writers like John partnered with secretaries and scribes to write their works as well.

While the Gospels were being completed, apostles and their close associates continued to compose epistles for churches throughout the Roman Empire. One of the last texts written by an eyewitness seems to have been the book of Revelation, an apocalypse penned by John during his exile on the island of Patmos.[26] The book of Revelation ends with a vision of Jesus Christ reigning with his Father over all creation and the Spirit inviting us to become part of this never-ending kingdom (Revelation 22:3, 17).

John was exiled on this island, still known as "Patmos" today, when he experienced the visions described in the book of Revelation.

From the moment that an apostolic text was written, it was regarded as authoritative (2 Thessalonians 2:15; 3:14).[27] No later than the second half of the first century, the apostles and eyewitnesses were already categorizing one another's writings as "Scripture" (2 Peter 3:15–16). Once the last eyewitnesses passed away, no more writings were received as authoritative because no more testimonies could come from Christ-commissioned witnesses of the resurrection.

In all of this, the Spirit of Christ was at work, inspiring the apostolic authors and safeguarding the words of these authors and their secretaries. We trust these texts still today because—in the words of Sinclair Ferguson—we believe that "the Father does not lie to his Son. The Son does not lie to the Spirit. The Spirit did not lie to the apostles … and the apostles did not lie to us."[28] In each of these texts, Jesus Christ remains the central focus; the goal is nothing less than a complete reorientation of our lives toward the kingdom of God in Christ.

Gospel

From Old English *godspel*, translation of Greek *euangelion*, "good news."

(1) gospel: Outside the New Testament in the first century AD, the word translated "gospel" referred to the proclamation of an event—such as a victory in battle or the rise of a new king—that changed the hearer's status and called for a response. In the New Testament, "gospel" came to mean the proclamation that the power of God's kingdom had entered human history through Jesus Christ to renew the whole world by means of his perfect life, substitutionary death, and victorious resurrection. When we trust what Jesus did—instead of what we can do—to be made right with God, God restores us to union with himself and communion with others.[29]

(2) Gospel: A text that narrates the life, death, and resurrection of Jesus Christ. The four New Testament Gospels belong in the category of ancient biographies and were clearly intended to be read as historical testimonies.[30]

Was It Like a Telephone Game? No—and Yes

So did the earliest testimonies about Jesus circulate like an empire-wide game of Telephone? Are the stories in the New Testament reliable testimonies? Or are they mangled fragments of truth, mingled with decades of myth and legend? Every evidence that survives today suggests these testimonies remained remarkably stable as they multiplied across the Roman Empire. And so, in one sense, the spread of the earliest testimonies about Jesus was nothing like the Telephone Game.

But there is one sense in which the spread of these testimonies was exactly like a game of Telephone.

The payoff at the end of a round of Telephone happens when the person who shared the first sentence compares the original message with the message that emerged at the end. The message that made its way around the circle can be corrected because the person with whom the message originated is still present in the circle.

That's precisely what happened with the oral histories that made their way into the New Testament.

If any testimony strayed from the truth, the testimony could be corrected because eyewitnesses were still circulating in the churches. Even when the final words in the New Testament were placed on papyrus in the late first century AD, at least a couple of eyewitnesses remained alive.[31] There was never a moment when the traditions that became part of the New Testament circulated as oral histories without living eyewitnesses available "in the circle" to correct any falsehoods.

"Don't Worry; I Read the Book. He Didn't Stay Dead."

The central claim of the New Testament is that Jesus was physically resurrected after being crucified. If this claim grew from decades of embellishment instead of historical truth, Jesus is dead, the apostles were liars, and our faith is vain (1 Corinthians 15:14–17). But evidences from the first and second centuries AD reveal that eyewitness testimony about Jesus emerged rapidly and circulated reliably. The New Testament texts relied on testimonies from apostolic eyewitnesses, and all of these texts were completed while the eyewitnesses were still alive. That's why we can say with confidence, "Don't worry; I read the book. He didn't stay dead."

Did Early Christians Care Whether the Events Described in the New Testament Really Happened?

According to some skeptics, early Christians didn't care whether or not they maintained accurate historical testimonies. "The first followers of Jesus," one such skeptic writes, "were not interested in preserving accurate memories of the historical person."[32] But texts from the first and second centuries AD demonstrate that early Christians did care deeply about preserving accurate memories—not only about Jesus but also about Paul and the other apostles.

Sometime in the second century AD, a text entitled *Acts of Paul* or *Journeys of Paul and Thecla* began to circulate in Asia Minor. This book was an extravagant tale that added a series of amazing adventures—and a sidekick named Thecla— to Paul's first missionary journey. In *Journeys of Paul and Thecla*, Thecla is condemned to die in an arena where she befriends a lioness and then leaps into a pool full of seals before being released. The stories are a little far-fetched, but some church members assumed that *Journeys of Paul and Thecla* preserved true testimonies from the life of Paul.

Now, if second-century Christians weren't concerned with preserving accurate testimonies, no one would have cared whether or not the tales in *Journeys of Paul and Thecla* were true—but, in fact, Christians did care about preserving the truth. That's why church leaders in Asia Minor investigated the origins of this book. What they discovered was that the stories in *Journeys of Paul and Thecla* were fiction. Their inquest led them to a pastor in Asia Minor. When questioned, the pastor-turned-novelist confessed he had passed off these stories as true testimonies—but he also said he'd concocted them "out of love for Paul."[33] Once the church leaders learned that he had written these fantasies, they forced the pastor to step down from his position.

If second-century Christians didn't care about true testimonies of what happened in history, why did this elder—who most likely wanted nothing more than to honor Paul's memory with a few super-fantastic tales—end up shamed and stripped of his ordination? From the first century forward, Christians knew that historical facts formed the basis for their faith and practices.

Chapter 5

Who Created the New Testament Canon?

- Christ-Commissioned Eyewitnesses
- The "Lost Gospels"
- Gnosticism

Imagine that you're a follower of Jesus at some point in the first two centuries of church history.

You have chosen to entrust your life to a deity who—according to the testimonies you've been taught—inaugurated God's kingdom on earth by dying on a cross and rising from the dead. You're fully aware that an emperor might, at any moment, renew the persecutions that began decades ago. And yet, in this despised sect known as the "Christians," you have found grace and peace like you've never experienced before. Through baptism, you've entered into a covenant with your fellow believers; their God has become your God, and their fate—whatever that may be—has become your fate. Now, you earnestly desire to learn everything you can about Jesus, this man who was also God.

But how?

There are no Christian bookstores in your local marketplace, after all. Even if you could purchase a scroll that contained Jesus' teachings, it wouldn't do you much good. Like the majority of men and women in the Roman Empire, you can't read or write.

Without easy access to writings about Jesus, how can you learn what your Savior said and did?

The capsa was an ancient cylindrical backpack designed to carry books.

Sure, you would interact with people in your church and learn testimonies from past believers—but most of your knowledge about Jesus would take shape each week as you listened to a literate believer read the Scriptures aloud.

"On the day called Sunday," a Christian named Justin wrote in the second century, "there is a gathering ... and the memoirs of the apostles or the writings of the prophets are read as long as time permits."[1]

The First Church Libraries

At first, Christians read from scrolls during these weekly gatherings—but that format changed quickly. No later than the early second century, another type of manuscript superseded scrolls in the churches: Sheets of papyrus began to be stacked, folded, and bound to form the "codex," the ancestor of the modern book.[2] Codexes were already popular prior to the dawn of

Christianity—but, before Christians came along, codexes were used mostly for legal notebooks and medical textbooks. Codexes enabled Christians to preserve all of Paul's letters in a single volume and to locate texts quickly.[3] And so, sometime in the first or early second century, Christians started copying in codex notebooks instead of rolled scrolls.

These copies of Scripture were so prized that early churches maintained libraries long before they owned buildings. If you were a Christian during the first few centuries of church history, your congregation would have kept copies of Scripture in an *armarion*,

Early medieval bookcase containing codexes

a special cabinet with niched shelves to hold scrolls and codexes. Such cabinets were common fixtures in Jewish synagogues and perhaps in the households of wealthy Romans.[4] Your church's cabinet would probably have remained in the home where your congregation assembled each week. Sometimes, Christians travelled and took their scrolls and codexes with them. When they did, they packed their books in a *capsa*—a backpack made from thin pieces of beechwood glued together to form a cylinder.[5]

By the mid-second century, your church's cabinet would probably have contained all four Gospels, the Acts of the Apostles, Paul's letters, at least one letter from John, and perhaps one letter from Peter and another from James. These writings were universally received as texts that conveyed the truth of God's new covenant—but there could also have been some writings whose standing was less certain. Your cabinet might have contained a series of visions that claimed to come from Simon Peter, for example, or a book that circulated under the title "The Shepherd." At least a few Christians had reservations about the Revelation to John, the epistle from Jude,

New Testament

The second part of the Christian Bible, which announces the fulfillment of God's Old Testament promises and the arrival of God's kingdom on earth through the perfect life, sacrificial death, and triumphant resurrection of Jesus Christ. The New Testament was originally written in Greek. "Testament" translates a Greek word that can also be rendered "covenant" (Luke 22:20; Hebrews 8:8-13).

85

and the second epistle ascribed to Peter; the letter to the Hebrews was still unknown in some regions.

Christians believed that God was inspiring new writings for his new covenant people—but how could they determine for certain which writings came from God and which ones didn't?

Manuscript of *The Shepherd*, included as an appendix in Codex Sinaiticus. *The Shepherd* was popular among early Christians. However, since it could not be traced to any apostolic witness, it was not received as Scripture. Tertullian pointed out that *The Shepherd* was "apocryphal" and not part of "the Divine Instrument" (Tertullian's term for the canonical Scriptures).[6]

If a text contradicted teachings that were known to have come from Jesus or the apostles, the solution was easy: the text shouldn't be received in the churches at all. But what about texts whose authorship was uncertain or ones that came after the time of the apostolic eyewitnesses? And what about epistles that claimed to come from apostles but couldn't be traced with confidence back to the ascribed authors? What should the churches do with these writings?

Why Christians Kept the Books They Kept

According to certain skeptics today, three centuries or more passed before Christians figured out which writings to receive and which ones to reject. Until that time—the skeptics claim—there was no consensus about which writings were authoritative. When Christians finally arrived at a consensus in the fourth or fifth century, what motivated them was not the preservation of truthful testimony about Jesus. Instead, Christians chose to keep the texts they kept and to suppress others in order to preserve the church's political power. Here are a few of the skeptics' claims:

✢ "The four gospels that made it into the official canon," atheist Richard Dawkins declares, "were chosen, more or less arbitrarily, out of a larger sample of at least a dozen."[7]

✢ "Many years passed before Christians agreed concerning which books should comprise their sacred Scriptures," an agnostic biblical scholar writes. "In part this was because other books were available, also written by Christians, many of their authors claiming to be the original apostles of Jesus."[8]

✤ "The Christian Bible" didn't emerge until after "the conversion of Constantine" in the early fourth century, says another skeptic.[9]

✤ Similar ideas have been popularized in novels like Dan Brown's *The Da Vinci Code*. A fictional scholar in this novel explains, "The modern Bible was compiled and edited by men who possessed a political agenda … to solidify their own power base."[10]

If these claims are true, the books in the New Testament were cherrypicked from a mongrel multitude of competing texts for the purpose of preserving the church's power.

But there's a problem with these skeptical claims.

The problem is that documents that survive from the first centuries of Christianity reveal a different story. Even in the first few decades of Christian history, a definite standard was already in place to discern which Christian texts were authoritative—and it wasn't an arbitrary coin-toss or a political power-play. *From the first century* AD *forward, the words of Christ-commissioned eyewitnesses were received as the words of Christ himself, and their writings were recognized as authoritative almost from the time they were written.*[11]

What's more, a core canon of undisputed texts—the four Gospels, Acts, the writings of Paul, and at least the first epistle from John—was well-established in the churches no later than the second century. It took some other writings longer to become well-known,[12] and Christians did debate the authenticity of a few texts. And yet, in time, Christians concluded together that a total of twenty-seven books—the texts that we know today as "the New Testament"—could be traced back to apostolic testimony from the first century AD. Christians kept the texts they kept because these texts could be traced back to eyewitnesses from the apostolic era.

To understand how this process unfolded, let's first take a look at some texts that didn't become part of the New Testament.

Nag Hammadi documents

Collection of more than forty Gnostic documents, unearthed in the mid-1940s near Nag Hammadi, a village in Upper Egypt. Significant texts found at Nag Hammadi include *Coptic Apocalypse of Paul*, *Coptic Apocalypse of Peter*, *Apocryphon of John*, *Dialogue of the Savior*, *Coptic Gospel of the Egyptians*, *Gospel of Philip*, *Gospel of Thomas*, and *Gospel of Truth*.

These are the writings that are sometimes dubbed "lost Gospels" or "lost Scriptures." What you'll discover is that early Christians did indeed exclude these texts—but not because Christians were scrambling to prop up their power structures! Early Christians rejected these writings because they were looking for trustworthy testimony about Jesus, and that's not what they found when they read the "lost Scriptures."

What are the "lost Gospels"?

The term "lost Gospels" usually refers to ancient writings that were excluded from the New Testament, even though they included supposed recollections of events and teachings from the life of Jesus. A few of these lost Gospels have lasted throughout the centuries. Others survive only in tiny fragments of papyrus or in brief quotations found in the writings of

Gospel of Thomas and The Secret Book of John, Codex II The Nag Hammadi manuscripts

early Christian scholars. Several lost Gospels were discovered anew in the past 100 years. Copies of some texts—such as *Gospel of Philip, Gospel of Thomas, Gospel of Truth,* and *Coptic Gospel of the Egyptians*—were unearthed in 1945 in Egypt, near a village known as Nag Hammadi.

If a *Gospel* is defined as an ancient retelling of the events or teachings from Jesus' life, there are fewer than thirty known Gospels. Unlike the New Testament Gospels, many of the lost Gospels record only isolated teachings or fragmentary incidents from the life of Jesus.

Why were the lost Gospels excluded from the New Testament?

The lost Gospels were excluded because they did not include reliable, eyewitness testimony about Jesus. Some scholars today depict this decision as having been made by powerful church leaders in the fourth century, three centuries after the books in the New Testament were written. One such scholar claims that a letter from a powerful bishop, Athanasius of Alexandria, declared the list of authoritative books in AD 367. He claims,

> *Athanasius wrote his annual pastoral letter to the Egyptian*
> *churches under his jurisdiction, and in it he included advice*

concerning which books should be read as Scripture in the churches. He lists our twenty-seven books, excluding all others. This is the first surviving instance of anyone affirming our set of books as the New Testament. And even Athanasius did not settle the matter. Debates continued for decades, even centuries.[13]

Each fact in this summary is *technically* correct, but it leaves out several key truths, leaving readers with these false impressions: (1) until the late fourth century, there was no consensus about which Christian writings were authoritative and true, and (2) even then, the church's standard was simply the authoritative statement of a powerful bishop.

So when *did* Christians agree on which writings were authoritative for their congregations? And what was the standard for this decision? Even in the first century AD, testimony that came from apostolic eyewitnesses of the risen Lord was considered to be uniquely authoritative. When the apostles and their associates began to write, their written interpretations of the gospel were every bit as authoritative as their spoken instructions. "If anyone does not obey our instruction in this letter," Paul said in his letter to the Thessalonians, "take special note of that person and do not associate with

> The lost Gospels were excluded because they couldn't be clearly connected to anyone who saw the resurrected Lord.

him" (2 Thessalonians 3:14). Before the end of the first century, Christians already referred to Paul's writings as "Scriptures" (2 Peter 3:15–16), and Paul himself cited words that would become part of Luke's Gospel as "Scripture" (Luke 10:7; 1 Timothy 5:18). Christians disagreed about whether a few texts in the New Testament could be clearly traced to apostolic eyewitnesses—but a clear standard existed from the very beginning. The lost Gospels were excluded because they couldn't be clearly connected to persons who walked and talked with Jesus.

Saint Athanasius, icon from Sozopol, Bulgaria

How Is Each Book in the New Testament Connected to a Christ-Commissioned Eyewitness?

Book	Author
Matthew	Matthew, apostle and eyewitness of the risen Lord (Matthew 9:9; 10:3; Acts 1:13)
Mark	Mark, traveling companion and translator for Simon Peter (1 Peter 1:13). "Mark, in his capacity as Peter's interpreter, wrote down accurately as much as he remembered" (Papias of Hierapolis, 2nd century).
Luke and Acts	Luke, traveling companion with Paul (Colossians 4:14; 2 Timothy 4:11). "Luke—the attendant of Paul—recorded in a book the Gospel that Paul declared" (Irenaeus of Lyon, 2nd century).
John	John, apostle and eyewitness of the risen Lord (Matthew 4:21; 10:2; Acts 1:13)
Romans, 1 and 2 Corinthians, Galatians, Ephesians, Philippians, Colossians, 1 and 2 Thessalonians, 1 and 2 Timothy, Titus, Philemon	Paul, apostle and later eyewitness of the risen Lord (1 Corinthians 9:1; 15:8–10). Some scholars deny that Paul authored some of these texts because of changes in the writing style; however, since Paul wrote these letters over a period of two decades and composed them with a secretary, a change in style does not necessarily indicate a change in authorship.
Hebrews	Received by early Christians as a proclamation from Paul or as a reliable reflection of Paul's theology written by someone else, based on the mention of Timothy (Hebrews 13:23). "Who wrote it, in truth, God only knows" (Origen of Alexandria, 3rd century).
James	James the Just, relative of Jesus and eyewitness of the risen Lord, recognized later as an apostle (Matthew 13:55; 1 Corinthians 15:7; Galatians 1:19; 2:9)

Book	Author
1 and 2 Peter	Peter, apostle and eyewitness of the risen Lord (Matthew 4:18; 10:2; Acts 1:13). Second Peter is so different from 1 Peter that many scholars deny that Peter wrote 2 Peter. It is possible that the shift between the two letters is due to different circumstances and different secretaries being involved in the composition of each letter.
1 John	John, apostle and eyewitness of the risen Lord (Matthew 4:21; 10:2; Acts 1:13)
2 and 3 John	John, apostle and eyewitness of the risen Lord (Matthew 4:21; 10:2; Acts 1:13). These epistles may have been written by another eyewitness named John, known as "John the elder," mentioned by Papias of Hierapolis (2nd century).
Jude	Jude, relative of Jesus and eyewitness of the risen Lord (Matthew 13:55)
Revelation	John, apostle and eyewitness of the risen Lord (Matthew 4:21; 10:2; Acts 1:13). It is possible, though unlikely, that Revelation was written by another eyewitness named John, known as "John the elder," mentioned by Papias of Hierapolis (2nd century).

Even while the New Testament books were being written, the words of people who saw and followed the risen Lord—specifically, the words and writings of the apostles—carried special weight in the churches (see Acts 1:21-26; 15:6–16:5; 1 Corinthians 4–5; 9:1–12; Galatians 1:1–12; 1 Thessalonians 5:26–27). After the apostles' deaths, Christians continued to cherish the testimony of eyewitnesses and their associates. Around AD 110, Papias of Hierapolis put it this way: "So, if anyone who had served the elders came, I asked about their sayings in detail—what Andrew or Peter said, or what was said by Philip or Thomas or James or John or Matthew or any other of the Lord's followers."[14] The people most likely to know the truth about Jesus were the ones who had encountered Jesus personally or the close associates of these witnesses. Although Christians did discuss a few writings for centuries, it was something much greater than political machinations that drove their decisions about which writings they received as authoritative. Their goal from the beginning was to receive the books that could be clearly connected to eyewitnesses of the risen Lord.

Only four Gospels—the ones known to us as the Gospels According to Matthew, Mark, Luke, and John—could be clearly connected to firsthand accounts of the risen Lord. Unlike the lost Gospels, each of the New Testament Gospels was written in the first century AD, at a time when the eyewitnesses of Jesus' ministry were still alive. What's more, it's possible to find evidence of widespread awareness among first- and second-century Christians that these Gospels represented eyewitness testimony.

✤ Papias of Hierapolis—a church leader in the geographic area known today as Turkey, born about the time the Gospels were being written and a friend of Philip's four daughters mentioned in Acts 21:9[15]— received his information about the first two New Testament Gospels from the first generation of Christians. According to Papias, the primary source for Matthew's Gospel was the testimony of Matthew, a follower of Jesus and former tax collector (Matthew 9:9).

✤ Papias also wrote that the author of Mark's Gospel had served as Peter's translator when Peter preached in the early churches. As such, what Mark recorded in his Gospel was the witness of Peter himself.[16]

✤ Shortly after the documents in the New Testament were completed, a pastor named Polycarp of Smyrna referred to the epistles of Paul as Scripture. Polycarp of Smyrna became a Christian in the first century and penned a letter to the church in Philippi around the year 110. In his letter, Polycarp identified Paul's letter to the Ephesians as Scripture: "As it is written in these Scriptures, 'Be angry and do not sin, and do not let the sun go down on your anger'" (Ephesians 4:26).[17]

✤ In a late second-century document known as the Muratorian Fragment, a church leader reports that Luke's Gospel came from Luke the physician who traveled with the apostle Paul.[18]

✤ The Muratorian Fragment also makes it clear that the apostle John was the source for the Gospel that bears John's name.

✤ In the second half of the second century, another church leader—Irenaeus of Lyons—reported that he had received these same traditions about the four Gospels from Christians of the first and second centuries.[19]

At least as early as the first and second centuries, it was widely recognized that the Gospels—now known by the names of Matthew, Mark, Luke, and John—represented eyewitness testimony about the life and ministry of Jesus Christ. In contrast, *none* of the lost Gospels can be connected to firsthand testimony.

Consistent and reliable testimonies have connected the names of Matthew, Mark, Luke, and John with these Gospels from the first century onward. Some scholars claim that the New Testament Gospels received their names in the same way that some of the lost Gospels received their titles—people wanted these writings to seem authoritative; so, they simply added names of eyewitnesses, even though these people really didn't write the Gospels at all. For example, one scholar puts it this way:

> *Sometime in the second century, when [Christians] recognized the need for apostolic authorities, they attributed these books to apostles (Matthew and John) and close companions of apostles (Mark, the secretary of Peter; and Luke the traveling companion of Paul).*[21]

How Many Gospels?

Some skeptics have suggested that hundreds of years passed before Christians settled on the four New Testament Gospels. Irenaeus of Lyon—a student of Polycarp, who had known the apostles—wrote less than a century after the last book of the New Testament was completed. By the time of Irenaeus, the New Testament Gospels were already a settled set of four: "The Gospels could not possibly be either more or less in number than they are. ... The Word himself ... gave us the gospel, fourfold in form but held together by one Spirit."[20]

The first problem with this skeptical line of thinking is that the Gospels According to Matthew, Mark, Luke, and John seem to have been connected with their authors as soon as the Gospels began to circulate widely. At this time, some people who knew the authors would still have been alive; under these circumstances, it would have been difficult to ascribe false names to the Gospels without raising questions among persons who knew the apostles and their close associates.

But there's another problem with the skeptics' claims: By the end of the first century, the four New Testament Gospels had circulated thousands of miles throughout the Roman Empire. In fact, a fragment of John's Gospel from the first half of the second century—a portion known as the John Rylands Papyrus Greek 457 or P52—has been found in Egypt, hundreds of miles from the Gospel's probable point of origin in Asia Minor.[22] Without rapid communication and without centralized church leadership, what would have happened if second-century Christians began ascribing false, apostolic names to the Gospels that had already spread this far from their places of origin? Most likely, each church would have connected a different author with each Gospel. Churches in Asia Minor might have ascribed a Gospel to the apostle Andrew, for example, while churches in Judea might have connected the same Gospel with Thaddeus or James or Jude. But, in every titled manuscript copy of the four New Testament Gospels, no matter what part of the world in which it was used, each Gospel is connected to the same author.

P52 (John Rylands Papyrus Greek 457) records portions of John 18.

Who created the New Testament canon?

No church council or bishop created the New Testament canon; instead, Christians recognized and received a canon that God created. This canon was breathed out by God as Christ-commissioned eyewitnesses and their close associates authored the books of the New Testament. A unanimous consensus emerged no later than the second century regarding the four Gospels, Acts, the letters of Paul, and at least the first letter from John. By the end of the fourth century, Christians had concluded that twenty-seven texts—the same texts found in your New Testament still today—could be traced back to apostolic eyewitnesses and their associates.

Canon

From Greek *kanon*, "measuring stick." Canon refers to religious texts that are authoritative for members of that particular religion. At least nineteen of the books in the New Testament were received as authoritative from the first and second centuries AD. This list of unquestioned books included the four Gospels, the Acts of the Apostles, the thirteen letters of Paul, and the first letter ascribed to John. Even if the New Testament had included only these books, every essential Christian doctrine would remain intact. In time, Christians recognized that Hebrews, James, 1 and 2 Peter, 2 and 3 John, Jude, and Revelation could also be connected to apostolic-era eyewitnesses.

Who wrote the lost Gospels?

No one knows for sure who wrote the lost Gospels. Even though the names of Jesus' apostles and other companions are attached to some of these supposed Gospels, no evidence exists to suggest that the authors of these texts even might have been eyewitnesses of the ministry of Jesus. In many cases, names such as "Mary" or "Philip" have been attached to these Gospels simply because these individuals are such prominent characters in the book. In a few instances—the *Gospel of Thomas*, for example—the Gospel does claim to come from a prominent apostle or church leader, but it is clear from the language used in the book that the document was written long after the death of its namesake.

Why were the lost Gospels written?

Some of the lost Gospels were later fanciful accounts of Jesus' life. Others were written to promote a theology that contradicted the eyewitness testimony found in the New Testament. A few—such as *Gospel of the Lord* and *Gospel of the Ebionites*—may have been variations of the New Testament Gospels, edited to fit the theology of certain sects. Still others—for example, *Infancy Gospel of Thomas*, *Infancy Gospel of James*, and perhaps *Gospel of Peter*—seem to have been penned by well-meaning Christians who felt compelled to expand stories in the New Testament. Many of these writings don't directly contradict anything in the New Testament, but they tend to expand the New Testament accounts in fanciful and problematic ways. For example, according to these writings, Jesus used his divine powers for his own benefit throughout his childhood.

The distinct theology of most of the lost Gospels was Gnostic. From the perspective of many Gnostics, the deity who created the universe was not the true or supreme God; the creator of the physical world was an evil deity, a rebel against a higher and greater deity. Since they understood the cosmos to be the product of an evil deity, most Gnostics viewed everything physical—including human sexuality and reproduction—as evil; many also claimed that Jesus Christ only seemed human. Since they were not particularly interested in the life of Jesus the man, the Gnostics focused most of their attention on other-worldly sayings and elaborate myths, some of which depicted biblical villains as heroes.

Gnostics

From Greek *ginoskein*, "to have knowledge." Gnostics were a sect that emerged within and separated from the Christian movement in the second century AD. Gnostics claimed to possess secret knowledge about God that was unavailable to others. Some Gnostics viewed the physical world and its Creator—usually identified with the God of the Old Testament—as evil. Many Gnostics were also *Docetists* (from Greek *dokein*, "to seem") who viewed Jesus not as God incarnate but as a divine spirit who *seemed* to possess a human body.

Why are so many people so enthralled by the lost Gospels?

Perhaps people long to believe that there's some knowledge or experience of Jesus Christ that isn't available in the words of the New Testament Gospels—and, in some sense, they're correct. There is experience and knowledge of Jesus Christ that isn't available simply by reading the New Testament as an artifact from the ancient past. But this deeper knowledge certainly is not available in the unreliable myths found in the lost Gospels! The full knowledge and experience that our souls crave happens as the Holy Spirit illumines our minds and we glimpse the all-surpassing glory of Jesus, the One in whom we are "made complete" and through whom we can enter into fellowship with the God who gives us his grace "far more abundantly beyond all that we ask or think" (Colossians 2:9–10; Ephesians 3:20).

Early Lists of Authoritative Christian Writings

Muratorian Fragment (late 2nd century)	Eusebius of Caesarea (early 4th century)	Athanasius of Alexandria (AD 367)
Received	**Received**	**Received**
Matthew	Matthew	Matthew
Mark	Mark	Mark
Luke	Luke	Luke
John	John	John
Acts	Acts	Acts
Romans	Romans	Romans
1 and 2 Corinthians	1 and 2 Corinthians	1 and 2 Corinthians
Galatians	Galatians	Galatians
Ephesians	Ephesians	Ephesians
Philippians	Philippians	Philippians
Colossians	Colossians	Colossians
1 and 2 Thessalonians	1 and 2 Thessalonians	1 and 2 Thessalonians
1 and 2 Timothy	1 and 2 Timothy	1 and 2 Timothy
Titus	Titus	Titus
Philemon	Philemon	Philemon
1 John	1 Peter	Hebrews
2 and 3 John (both letters counted as one)	1 John	James
Jude	Revelation	1 and 2 Peter
Revelation of John		1, 2, and 3 John
Wisdom of Solomon	**Disputed**	Jude
	Hebrews	Revelation
Received by some but not all	James	
Revelation of Peter	Jude	
	2 Peter	
Hebrews, James, 1 Peter, and 2 Peter are not mentioned. It is possible that the reference to Revelation of Peter was originally a reference to one of Peter's letters but has been misunderstood.	2 and 3 John	
	Eusebius later referred to Revelation as a book "which some reject but others classify with the received books."	

How the Bible
Made It from
Manuscripts to You

On July 17 in the year 180, twelve Christians from the North African village of Scillium were dragged into the presence of the Roman proconsul. Christian faith was a capital crime at this time, and the Roman emperor Marcus Aurelius had recently launched a new wave of persecution.

The proconsul begged the Christians to save themselves from death: "You can gain the pardon of our lord the emperor, if you will only return with a sound mind! Our religion is simple: we swear by the genius of our lord the emperor and pray for his welfare. So should you."

"I do not recognize the empire of this world. I serve the God whom no human being has seen," a Christian named Speratus replied. "I've committed no theft; I pay taxes on all that I purchase. I do all this because I know my Lord; he alone is the King of all kings and the Emperor over every nation."

The proconsul pressed Speratus further: "What do you have in your *capsa?*" A *capsa* was an ancient backpack built to carry books. Even in this early era of church history, Christians cherished and carried particular written texts.

"Books," Speratus replied, "and the letters of Paul, a righteous man."

The "books" in his backpack most likely included the four Gospels and perhaps Acts. If so, Speratus was carrying most of the New Testament with him.[1] Despite repeated opportunities to recant, Speratus and his companions refused to recant the truths written in their Scriptures. When they received their death sentences, the twelve replied, "Thanks be to God! This day, we will be witnesses in heaven." And so they were.

This wasn't the last time that ancient Christians were asked about their books. In fact, when a later emperor wanted to obliterate Christianity completely, he issued an edict not only to seek out Christian leaders but also to burn the Christian Scriptures.[2] The Scriptures were crucial for the survival of Christian faith, and even the movers and shakers of the Roman Empire knew it. The church cannot survive for long without the Scriptures.

One consequence of the church's rootedness in the written Word of God is that increased literacy has closely followed the spread of Christianity. Ancient and medieval Christian missionaries were the ones who "introduced the technologies of reading and writing into the oral cultures of Europe."[3] And so, when men like John Wycliffe and William Tyndale worked to make the Scriptures accessible to every English-speaking person, they were continuing a long tradition of Christian literacy.

In this section, you'll learn how God preserved his written Word from ancient times to today. You will see how copyists reproduced the text reliably. Then, you'll learn about monks and scholars and pastors who translated the Scriptures into English, sometimes at the cost of their lives.

Even in the earliest stages of Christian history, Christians have been known as people who treasured and taught from written texts.

Chapter 6

How Was the New Testament Copied?

- Manuscript Differences
- Textual Criticism
- Earliest Copies

Elijah had a problem with his Bible—or so he thought.[1]

One of my partners in this project, Elijah, described to me a faith-shaking moment that marked his college years.

Elijah was part of an evangelistic ministry and spent a lot of time sharing his faith with people at the mall or before football games. Many of these people had questions about Christianity; once in a while, someone even had a question about the Trinity. Elijah thought he had found the perfect Bible verse about the Trinity to share with these people: "For there are three that bear record in heaven: the Father, the Word, and the Holy Spirit; and these three are one" (1 John 5:7). This verse made it crystal clear that God was one and yet three.

Everything went well until one day, a friend—a Bible-believing Christian, no less—told Elijah, "You've got to stop using that verse."

Imagine that! Elijah had the perfect verse right in front of him in his Bible, and he was being told not to use it.

"You have to use other verses in the Bible to show that Jesus is God," his friend told him. "But you can't use that one, because it wasn't in the original text. It was added into Bibles later. It wasn't there when John wrote his letter."

Elijah was crushed.

No one had ever told him that there were differences in the ancient copies of the Bible. Now that he knew about these disagreements, he wondered, how could he trust the Bible at all? How was he supposed to know when a text had been changed?

Maybe you've had a similar experience.

Perhaps you were reading the Lord's Prayer at a Bible study and discovered that your Bible ends the prayer with a phrase like this one: "for thine is the kingdom, the power, and the glory, for ever and ever. Amen." The person sitting next to you, however, doesn't have those words in her

Bible at all! Or maybe you were reading through the book of John and noticed a footnote in your Bible saying that some ancient manuscripts didn't include John 7:53–8:11. Perhaps you, like Elijah, wondered, "How can I know which reading is right?"

Well, in time, Elijah did end up finding the answers to his questions—and so can you.

The answers are in the manuscripts.

What If the Copies Are Corrupted?

Suppose you own a Bible, but it's translated in a style that's difficult to understand. Or maybe your Bible has simply worn out from years of usage. If so, you can easily walk into any Christian bookstore and pick up a different version of the Bible.

The earliest Christians couldn't do that.

There was no "Polycarp Standard Version" or "Saint James Study Bible with Limited Edition Camel-Knee Binding" on anyone's bookshelf, and there were no printing presses or photocopy machines. Early Christians read the Scriptures from codexes and scrolls. These copies of the Scriptures were hand-written from whatever manuscripts the copyists happened to possess when a copy was needed. And so, it was crucial for copyists to reproduce these texts accurately.

A copyist's life was a hard one—or at least that's what some copyists thought. Here are a few comments that copyists left in the texts they copied: "Writing is excessive drudgery. It crooks your back, it dims your sight, it twists your stomach and your sides. ... As the sick man desires health even so does the scribe desire the end of the volume."[2]

But did they?

Certain skeptics give the impression that ancient copyists changed the biblical texts in ways that ought to worry Christians today. Here's how one agnostic scholar describes the status of the New Testament manuscripts:

> *Not only do we not have the originals [of the Greek manuscripts of the New Testament], we don't have the first copies of the originals.*

... What we have are copies made later—much later. ... These copies differ from one another in so many places that we don't even know how many differences there are. ... Christianity ... is a textually oriented religion whose texts have been changed, surviving only in copies that vary from one another, sometimes in highly significant ways.[3]

Such statements suggest that the process of copying the Scriptures worked something like the Telephone Game (much like skeptics have depicted the oral histories you learned about in a previous chapter). In the Telephone game, of course, you might start with "I like pepperoni pizza" but end up with "Don't let the purple aliens build pyramids when the zombies attack." Could it be that the verses in the New Testament have been similarly corrupted by careless copyists? If so, even if the original New Testament texts told the truth, how can we be sure that what we read in the New Testament today is true, since it may have changed over the centuries? Has the message of Jesus been lost in transmission?

Textual Criticism

The analysis of various copies, fragments, versions, and translations of a text with the goal of recovering the wording of the original manuscript in its final form.[5]

Truth be told, the skeptics' claims are overblown. The New Testament has not changed significantly over the centuries, and nothing essential to the message of Jesus has been lost in transmission.[4] In the first place, manuscripts weren't copied a single time and then tossed aside, like the individual sentences whispered around the circle in a Telephone Game. Manuscripts were kept, repeatedly copied, and sometimes used to check later copies.

How Can the Bible Be Inerrant If the Copyists Made Mistakes?

Inerrancy refers to the *original autographs* of Scripture, not to every copy made afterward. God inspired the authors of Scripture and safeguarded their words from error, and so the original autographs were inerrant. God did *not*, however, choose to prevent the thousands of copyists across the ages from making mistakes as they copied Scripture. The surviving copies of Scripture are sufficiently accurate for us to recover the inerrant truth that God intended and inspired, but they have not always been copied with perfect accuracy.

What's more, textual critics today don't start with the manuscripts left over at the end of the copying process, like the last sentence uttered in the Telephone Game. The Greek text that stands behind today's New Testament is the result of careful reconstruction using the earliest surviving manuscripts, not a few leftovers at the end!

In this chapter, you'll learn that, yes, copyists made mistakes, and some copyists even altered texts. And yet, such lapses were relatively rare. Copyists worked hard to keep their copies correct and, for the most part, they got it right. Even when they didn't get it right, most of their mistakes were mere misspellings or slips of the pen—variants that are easy to spot and easily corrected. When it comes to more difficult variants, so many manuscripts and fragments of the New Testament have survived that scholars can almost always reconstruct the original reading of the text. In those few instances where uncertainty about the right reading remains, none of the possibilities changes anything that Christians believe about God or about his work in the world.

Scriptio Continua

Certain skeptics like to point out that early copyists were dealing with what's known as *scriptio continua*—texts that included no punctuation and no spaces.[6] (If you don't think spaces between words matter, consider this sentence: youarenowhere. Are you "now here" or "nowhere"? Or how about this one: lastnightisawabundanceonthetable. Does this sentence describe a usual or an unusual event? An "abundance" of food on the table happens all the time, after all. But "a bun dance on the table"? Not so much—not on my dining room table, anyway!) *Scriptio continua* does not mean, however, that manuscripts had no spaces or punctuation whatsoever. It simply means that they didn't use spaces and punctuation like we have today. Even in the early New Testament manuscripts, there were punctuation markers, paragraph divisions, and occasional marks to show when a new word starts. Furthermore, ancient copyists and readers were familiar with this form of writing, so they were quite capable of copying and reading *scriptio continua* accurately.

Many Manuscripts Means Many Variants

So did copyists make changes in the manuscripts?

Of course they did!

The copyists were human beings, and being human means making mistakes. Since God chose not to override their humanity as they copied the New Testament, these human beings were every bit as prone to short attention spans, poor eyesight, and fatigue as you or me. They had no eyeglasses or contact lenses to sharpen their vision, and they relied on the flickering light of lamps to see.

Since God did not "re-inspire" the text each time it was reproduced, sometimes the copyists miscopied their sources. Once in a while, they even tried to fix things that weren't broken by changing words that they thought a heretic might misconstrue.[7] The result is hundreds of thousands of copying variants scattered among the New Testament manuscripts.

One popular skeptic's much-repeated soundbite is that "there are more variations among our manuscripts than there are words in the New Testament"; this statement is technically true but—unless his listeners are aware of the vast number of New Testament manuscripts that survive today—it's also a bit misleading.[8] There are around 138,000 words in the Greek New Testament, and hundreds of thousands of variants can be found scattered among the Greek manuscripts— but that number of variants comes from adding up *every difference* in *every surviving manuscript* from the Greek New Testament.[9] Well over 5,000 Greek New Testament manuscripts have been preserved as a whole or in part—more than any other text from the ancient

The reason there are so many variants among the Greek manuscripts of the New Testament is because so many manuscripts have survived— well over 5,000 manuscripts, in whole or in part! But having so many manuscripts also means that scholars are able to reconstruct the original text with an extremely high degree of accuracy.

"The interval between the dates of the original composition and the earliest extant evidence [is] so small as to be negligible, and the last foundation for any doubt that the Scriptures have come down to us substantially as they were written has now been removed."—Frederic Kenyon, Director of the British Museum, 1909-1931[13]

world![10] With so many surviving manuscripts, it doesn't take long for the number of variants to exceed the number of words in the Greek New Testament.

If only one manuscript of the New Testament had survived, there would have been zero variants (and this single manuscript would probably have become an idol to which people would make pilgrimages today!). But early Christians believed that all of God's Word should be accessible to all of God's people. And so, every church seemed to have possessed its own codexes of apostolic texts—and that's why more than 5,000 whole or partial manuscripts survive today.

Codex Robertsonianus, 11th century AD. Acquired by Greek scholar A. T. Robertson in 1927, this manuscript is a *minuscule*—a text written in lower-case letters. The splotch may be the result of someone spilling liquid on the page, perhaps while celebrating the Lord's Supper. (Photo courtesy of Southern Seminary)

Spread across millions and millions of words in more than 5,000 manuscripts, the variations represent a small percentage of the total text. According to one scholar, the New Testament text is 92.6% stable.[11] In other words, all these differences affect less than 8% of the New Testament text! What's more, the overwhelming majority of these differences have to do with words that are misspelled or rearranged—differences that have no impact on the translation or meaning of the text.[12] What this means practically is that the text of the New Testament has been sufficiently preserved for us to recover the words that God intended and inspired. What's more, several portions of the New Testament survive from the second century—a century or less after the time when God first inspired eyewitnesses of the risen Lord to write!

The New Testament is, in fact, the best preserved text from the ancient world—better than the writings of Homer, Herodotus, or even Plato.

Works of Plato	New Testament
• Written around 400 BC.	• Written between AD 49 and 96.
• Only 210 copies have survived.	• Well over 5,000 portions have survived.
• The earliest surviving manuscript was copied in AD 895, more than 1,200 years after the original documents were written.	• Fragments survive from a few decades after the texts were first written.
	• Complete books survive from the 2nd century, less than a century after the books were written.
	• Complete manuscripts of the New Testament survive from the early 4th century, less than three centuries after the original documents were written.

"The wealth of material that is available for determining the wording of the original New Testament is staggering: more than fifty-seven hundred Greek New Testament manuscripts, as many as twenty thousand versions, and more than one million quotations by patristic writers. In comparison with the average ancient Greek author, the New Testament copies are well over a thousand times more plentiful. If the average-sized manuscript were two and one-half inches thick, all the copies of the works of an average Greek author would stack up four feet high, while the copies of the New Testament would stack up to over a *mile* high! This is indeed an embarrassment of riches."—Daniel Wallace[14]

With that in mind, let's take a look together at the different types of variants found in the New Testament manuscripts. After that, we'll learn about a few important Greek manuscripts and examine the textual variants in one of the most famous verses in the New Testament.

What Kinds of Changes Did Copyists Make?

Variant	Description	Importance/Example
Nonsense	Simple copying mistake resulting in a phrase that clearly doesn't make sense, typically easy to recognize and to correct	In one manuscript, for example, Galatians 1:11 begins, "For I would have you know, brethren, that the gospel the gospel the gospel...." Clearly, this copyist was serious about the gospel—either that, or he accidentally copied a phrase two extra times and thus introduced an easily-corrected variant into the text.
Change in spelling	Alternatively spelled word, typically easy to recognize and to correct	These variants rarely affect the translation or the meaning. Most often, the spelling errors are simply spelling variations, similar to the difference between the American form of the word "color" and British form, "colour." Even when actual spelling errors may have occurred, the meaning of the text hasn't changed. Even in English, misspellings don't change the meaning. (Yoo kould stil unnderstand teh meening off ah sentense, evven iff evry wurd happned two bee mispelled!)
Change in word order	Some words rearranged	Word order does not matter as much in Greek as in English; changes in Greek word order do not affect the meaning or the translation of the text. (Of Yoda you must think, and make more sense it will.)

Variant	Description	Importance/Example
Substitution	Word or phrase changed to another word or phrase	Substitutions were sometimes accidental, sometimes intentional, but they rarely change the meaning of the text. For example, in some manuscripts, John 1:6 reads, "There came a man sent from God," while a few have, "There came a man sent from the Lord." A word has changed but the meaning remains the same.
Harmonization	Change to make one text more similar to a nearby text or to a parallel passage in another book	In many manuscripts, for example, the Lord's Prayer in Luke's Gospel (11:2-4) is expanded to sound more like the Lord's Prayer in Matthew's Gospel (6:9-13). The point of the prayer remains unchanged, and nothing is introduced that would change our beliefs about God or about his work in the world. Since copyists copied the four Gospels consecutively, it's not surprising that they sometimes adapted phrases from one Gospel to sound like a similar text in another Gospel.
Addition	Addition of a word, phrase, or section to the source text	Sometimes, copyists felt compelled to explain a custom that later readers might not know (John 5:3-4, for example, is added to explain the custom at the pool) or to include a well-known narrative (John 7:53-8:11 was added to John's Gospel hundreds of years after the Gospel was completed). Once again, these changes do not affect what we believe about God or about his work in the world.

Variant	Description	Importance/Example
Omission	Word or phrase left out of the text, usually accidentally	One copyist, for example, accidentally left out the Greek word in John 3:16 that's translated "he gave." In this particular instance, the copyist caught his own omission and corrected it—but sometimes copyists didn't catch their omissions, resulting in variants in the manuscripts.
Theological change	Change to emphasize a particular theological truth or to prevent misuse of a text by heretics	Theological changes were more the exception than the rule. A very clear pattern of changes would be needed to prove that the changes were theological. If there is no pattern, the scribe may have just made mistakes that happened to be theological. The addition of 1 John 5:7 in the Latin Bible could be an example of a change intended to emphasize a particular theological truth.

Codex Vaticanus, 4th century AD. When one copyist changed the wording in Codex Vaticanus, a later copyist rewrote the original word and added this marginal note (shown here): "Fool and knave! Leave the old reading, don't change it."

A Fresh Look at a Familiar Verse

"JOHN 3:16." When you see the sign at sporting events, it's *not* because someone is searching for a friend named John who was supposed to be sitting in row 3, seat 16. It's an attempt to point people to a particular Bible verse that beautifully summarizes the gospel: "For God so loved the world, that He gave His only begotten Son that whoever believes in Him should not perish, but have eternal life" (John 3:16).

Now, you've probably read John 3:16 at some point in your life; some of you may even have memorized this verse. But did you know that there are variants in the Greek manuscripts of this verse? Here's a rough—almost word-for-word—translation of John 3:16 from four different Greek manuscripts. The differences you see in the English translations show the differences that you would see if you studied this verse in the Greek manuscripts.[15]

Papyrus 66 (Around AD 200 or later)	For in this way God loved the world, that the Son—the one and only—he gave so that everyone who believes in him would not perish, but would have eternal life.
Papyrus 75 (Around AD 200)	For in this way God loved the world, that the Son—the one and only—he gave so that everyone who believes **upon** him would not perish, but would have eternal life.
Codex Sinaiticus (original reading, 4th century)	For in this way God loved the world, that the Son—the one and only—[]so that everyone who believes in him would not perish, but would have eternal life.
Codex Sinaiticus (corrected readings, 4th and 7th centuries)	For in this way God loved the world, that the Son **his**—the one and only—**he gave** so that everyone who believes in him would not perish, but would have eternal life.
Codex Alexandrinus (5th century)	For in this way God loved the world, that the Son **his**—the one and only—he gave so that everyone who believes in him **is not perishing**, but would have eternal life.

So what kinds of variants do we see in John 3:16?

✤ **Substitution**: The copyist of Papyrus 75 substituted "upon" for "in."

The copyist of Codex Alexandrinus changed the verb tense from "perish" to "perishing."

+ **Addition or Correction of Omission**: The Greek word that means "his" is included in Codex Alexandrinus. Around 300 years after Codex Sinaiticus was originally copied, another copyist added this same word in Codex Sinaiticus. "The Son his" sounds awkward in English, but it's a common construction in Greek that would be translated into English as "his Son."

+ **Omission**: The scribe who copied Codex Sinaiticus (original reading) left out the Greek word that means "he gave"—but then he caught and corrected his own mistake. Take a look at the manuscript, and you'll notice how this mistake happened:

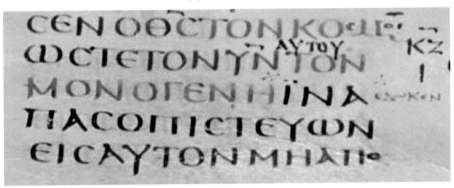

Do you see how the ink grows lighter leading up to the word that looks like "INA," then suddenly the ink grows dark again? That's the spot in the manuscript where the copyist left out the Greek word that means "he gave"—and it seems clear what happened. The copyist ran out of ink. When he re-inked his pen, he lost his place and left out a word.[16] Then, he saw his mistake and fixed it.

Notice the tiny word written in the right margin, with sign above it that looks sort of like a percent sign? That's the missing Greek word that means "he gave"; the same sign appears between the lines in the text before "INA," to show the reader where in the sentence the word belongs.

Uncial

Uncial is a writing script commonly used in manuscripts from the fourth until the eighth century AD. Uncial scripts are written in *majuscule* (all upper-case letters). Many important manuscripts of the New Testament—including Codex Sinaiticus and Codex Vaticanus—were copied in uncial script.

(If you're wondering about those red letters, this wasn't a red-letter Bible. It's an ancient cross-referencing system that helped readers to track down parallel passages in other Gospels.) A different "corrector" working about 300 years later also added "AYTOY"—the Greek word that means "his"—between the lines.

Now, notice how none of these textual variants changes the meaning of this verse! With or without the word "his," it's obvious that the "Son" in John 3:16 is God's Son. The point of the verse is identical in every manuscript: God showed his love for the world by sending his Son to save believers from perishing and to give them unending life.

So how much do these variants impact our English translations of the Bible? In truth, not very much at all! Most differences in English translations of the Bible aren't because of differences in Greek manuscripts; they're due to different approaches to the task of translating the Bible. Take a look at the same verse in five different English translations:

Bible Version	John 3:16
King James Version	For God **so** loved the world, that he gave his **only begotten** Son that **whosoever believeth** in him **should** not perish, but have **everlasting** life.
New International Version	For God **so** loved the world that he gave his **one and only** Son that **whoever believes** in him **shall** not perish but have **eternal** life.
Holman Christian Standard Bible	For God loved the world **in this way**: He gave His **One and Only** Son so that **everyone who believes** in Him **will** not perish but have **eternal** life.
English Standard Version	For God **so** loved the world, that he gave his **only** Son that **whoever believes** in him should not perish but have **eternal** life.
New American Standard Bible	For God **so** loved the world, that He gave His **only begotten** Son that **whoever believes** in Him should not perish, but have **eternal** life.

Notice that the English translations differ far more than the Greek manuscripts! The most noticeable difference in the English translations is whether Jesus should be called God's "only Son," "one and only Son," or "only begotten Son"—but that's not due to a difference in the manuscripts. All of the Greek manuscripts have the precise same words at this point! Those are three different ways to translate the same Greek word into English.

Where Did that *Comma* Come From?

So what about that clause in 1 John 5:7 that Elijah once used to prove the Trinity?

Sometime before the end of the fourth century, someone seems to have included this comment about the Trinity when copying a Latin text of 1 John: "There are three that bear witness in heaven: the Father, the Word, and the Holy Spirit; and these three are one" (5:7).[17] Over time, these words ended up being included in the Latin text of 1 John. In ancient Greek, the word *comma* means "short clause," so this added comment has become known as *Comma Johanneum* or "Comma from John's [Writings]."

The "comma" is certainly true; the Father, the Word (Jesus, the Son), and the Spirit *are* three and yet one. Still, the clause wasn't part of John's original letter. In fact, not even one ancient Greek manuscript includes the *Comma Johanneum*. The first Greek manuscript to include it was copied more than a millennium after John's letter was written.[18] But the church's teaching about the Trinity has never depended on the *Comma Johanneum*. The Great Commission in Matthew's Gospel states the concept of one God ("in the *name*," singular) in three persons ("of the Father and of the Son and of the Holy Spirit") no less clearly than this clause that someone added to 1 John (Matthew 28:19–20).

And what about that additional line in the Lord's Prayer? At some point very early in the church's history, Christians began appending a paraphrased snippet from 1 Chronicles 29:11 when they recited the Lord's Prayer: "For yours is the kingdom and power and glory forever. Amen." Eventually, this addition became so familiar that a copyist included it when copying Matthew's Gospel. Still later, other copyists expanded the version of the Lord's Prayer that's found in the eleventh chapter of Luke's Gospel to fit the more-familiar version in Matthew's Gospel. Once again, the addition is true and taught elsewhere in Scripture. And, once again, the textual variant changes nothing that we believe about God or about his work in the world.

Considering the Copyists

Elijah had thought he had a problem with his Bible, but he didn't have a problem with the Bible at all. He had a problem with his understanding of how we got the Bible. Once he learned how many copies we have, how early they were copied, and how well the text was preserved, he saw that there was no reason for the differences among the manuscripts to shake his faith—in fact, learning all of this ultimately increased his trust in the reliability of Scripture.

We are deeply indebted to those early copyists of Scripture. Many risked their lives making or saving copies of the New Testament. We may never know how many ancient Christians gave their lives trying to save those copies of Scripture. The Bibles that we have today are as reliable as they are because the early copyists preserved the text of the New Testament so well. We have their manuscripts. They should have our gratitude.

What Are the Some of the Most Important Early Copies of the Greek New Testament?[19]

Manuscript	Description	Date
P52 (Papyrus Rylands Greek 457)	Fragment from a copy of John's Gospel (18:31–33, 37–38)	2nd century AD
P90 (Papyrus Oxyrhynchus 3523)	Fragment from a copy of John's Gospel (18:36–19:1; 19:2–7)	2nd century AD
P104 (Papyrus Oxyrhynchus LXIV 4404)	Fragment from a copy of Matthew's Gospel (21:34–37; 21:45)	2nd century AD
P64 (Magdalen Papyrus) P67 P4	Fragments from a codex of the four Gospels (Matthew 3:9–15; 5:20–28; 26:7–33; Luke 1:58–2:7; 3:8–4:2; 4:29–35; 5:3–8; 5:30–6:16). Demonstrates that the New Testament Gospels were being copied together very early.	2nd or 3rd century AD
P98	Fragment from a copy of Revelation (1:13–2:1)	2nd or 3rd century AD

Manuscript	Description	Date
P103 (Papyrus Oxyrhynchus 4403)	Fragment from a copy of Matthew's Gospel (13:55–56; 14:3–5)	2nd or 3rd century AD
P75 (Hanna Papyrus 1 Mater Verbi; Papyrus Bodmer XIV-XV)	Portions from a manuscript that included Luke's and John's Gospels (Luke 3:18–John 15:8). Corrections in the manuscript show early copyists' concern for complete accuracy.	Around AD 200
P66 (Papyrus Bodmer II)	Codex of John's Gospel. Corrections in the manuscript show early copyists' concern for complete accuracy.	Probably around AD 200, perhaps as late as the 4th century AD
P46 (Papyrus Chester Beatty II)	Portions from a manuscript that included Paul's epistles and Hebrews arranged in order of decreasing length. First and Second Timothy as well as Titus were not included in this manuscript, perhaps because those letters were addressed to individuals not churches. It is unknown whether the original manuscript included Philemon.	Around AD 200
P45 (Papyrus Chester Beatty I)	Portions from a manuscript that included all four Gospels and Acts collected and copied together (Matthew 20–21; 25–26; Mark 4–9; 11–12; Luke 6–7; 9–14; John 4–5; 10–11; Acts 4–17). Copyist sometimes smoothed or paraphrased wording while remaining true to the original meaning.	3rd century AD

Manuscript	Description	Date
Codex Sinaiticus (א, 01)	Oldest complete copy of the New Testament. Includes all the books in the New Testament, as well as two additional texts copied after Revelation: *Epistle of Barnabas* and *The Shepherd*. Discovered at St. Catherine's Monastery near Mount Sinai.	4th century AD
Codex Alexandrinus (A, 02)	Near-complete copy of the Old and New Testaments in Greek. Portions of the Gospels and of Paul's letters have not survived.	4th or 5th century AD
Codex Vaticanus (B, 03)	Near-complete codex of the Old and New Testaments in Greek. Includes some Old Testament apocryphal texts. Codex Vaticanus has been in the Vatican Library as long as the records go back. Both P75 and Codex Vaticanus may be traced back to a single late second-century manuscript from which the textual predecessors of Codex Vaticanus were copied. Since a century and a half separates these two manuscripts and yet they remain very similar, it is clear that copyists maintained a high level of accuracy in their copies.	4th century AD

Manuscript	Description	Date
Codex Ephraemi Rescriptus (C, 04)	Bible codex that was erased and reused to preserve the sermons of a preacher named Ephraem the Syrian, hence the name "Ephraemi Rescriptus" ("of Ephraim, rewritten"). Parchment was expensive, so instead of purchasing more parchment, scribes sometimes scraped the ink off old manuscripts and reused the codex as a new book. These codexes are called "palimpsests" (from Greek, *palin* ["again"] + *psestos* ["rubbed smooth"]). Most of the New Testament survives. Enough traces of ink remain on this codex to read the original Greek, aided by chemicals and special photography. A. T. Robertson, a famous Greek scholar, once commented regarding this codex, "It is not the only time that sermons have covered up the Bible, alas."	5th century AD
Codex Bezae (D, 05) Also known as Codex Cantabrigiensis	Dual-language manuscript of the Gospels and Acts, with Greek on the left-hand pages and Latin on the right. Once belonged to a French scholar and pastor named Theodore Beza. Particularly in Acts, the text has been altered at times to distinguish Christianity more clearly from Judaism.	5th century AD

Chapter 7

Where Did the English Bible Come From?

- Bible Translation
- John Wycliffe
- William Tyndale
- The King James Version

The Bible wasn't written in English. In fact, when the Bible was written, English didn't even exist! The Scriptures were composed in Hebrew, Aramaic, and Greek. And so, if you own a Bible in English, it's because someone translated the Scriptures for you.

But you probably already knew that.

What you may *not* know is that owning an English Bible was once hazardous to your health. Six hundred years ago, you could be burned at the stake for producing or possessing an English Bible. From the perspective of many church leaders in this era, Bible translation and heresy went hand in hand; the Scriptures had to remain in Latin, only to be read by trained clergy.[1] And so, if you possess

Bede dictating his translation of John's Gospel.

an English Bible today, you owe a debt of gratitude to thousands of men and women who risked their lives to make the Bible available in English.

In this chapter, you'll learn about a few of the Christians who translated the Scriptures into English. In the process, you'll meet a monk who died dictating a translation of John's Gospel, a priest who was burned at the stake decades after he was already dead, and a man whose last breath was a prayer asking God to open the eyes of a king.

Our story of the English Scriptures begins with a cow-herding monk singing in a field in North Yorkshire, hundreds of years before the English Bible became illegal.[2]

Caedmon, the Original Singing Cowboy

Nearly seven centuries after the Holy Spirit empowered the first disciples in Jerusalem, a cow-herding monk named Caedmon began singing the storyline of Scripture in English. Caedmon started with the creation of the world and sang his way through the coming of the Holy Spirit. None of Caedmon's original songs have survived to us today and they weren't exactly translations of the Bible, but the songs that Caedmon sang in the fields of England marked the beginning of a tradition of making Scripture accessible in English.[3]

The Monk Who Died in the Middle of John's Gospel

A few years after Caedmon started singing the storyline of Scripture, another monk began translating Scripture into Old English. This monk's name was Bede. What bothered Bede was that many pastors didn't know enough Latin to understand the Bible or to teach the Bible to their people. At the very least, Bede wanted anyone whom the church ordained for ministry to know the Apostles' Creed and the Lord's Prayer in English, but Bede didn't stop with a mere creed and a prayer. He longed for pastors to be able to understand the Word of God for themselves; so, Bede began translating bits of the Latin Vulgate Bible into English. Even on his deathbed, Bede kept dictating the Scriptures in English. His last words were a translation of John 6:9: "But what are they among so many?"[4]

Glossy Bibles and the End of Old English

None of Bede's translations have survived, but it's quite likely that they were "glosses." Glossing the Bible sounds to people today like Bede may have polished his Bible or applied polyurethane until the pages were particularly shiny, but that wasn't at all what glossing meant in the Middle Ages! Glosses were word-by-word renderings of the Latin Vulgate, usually with each English word written immediately above the Latin word. The result was awkward English, but it was enough to help clergy understand the words they were reading in Latin.

In the late ninth century, Alfred—the king of the West Saxons—was doing more than merely glossing the Bible. King Alfred had portions from the Old Testament turned into Old English prose, and he incorporated these translations into his code of law. Alfred himself translated the first fifty psalms from Latin into Old English, and he

Lindisfarne Gospels

The Lindisfarne Gospels were copied in Latin in the early eighth century. In the tenth century, the Gospels were glossed in Old English; the glosses in the Lindisfarne Gospels are the oldest surviving translation of the Gospels into English.

125

faced a dilemma that translators still face today: How tightly should a translation be tied to the original language? Should the translation be word for word or idea for idea? Alfred's solution was simple, if not particularly helpful: "Sometimes I translated word for word, sometimes sense for sense."[5]

A century after Alfred translated his psalms, a scholar named Aelfric continued this tradition and helped to turn the first seven books of the Old Testament into Old English. Aelfric placed a high value not only on translating the Scriptures but also on proclaiming the Scriptures in sermons.

It was in one of his sermons that Aelfric declared, "Happy is he ... who reads the Scriptures if he convert the words into actions." And yet, when Aelfric spoke these words, the vast majority of English-speaking people *couldn't* convert the words of Scripture into action because they never heard the Scriptures in a language they could understand. They heard the Bible only in Latin, and no one seems to have considered the possibility of providing ordinary people with the Scriptures.[6]

These first small steps toward a complete English Bible lurched to a halt in 1066. That's when Duke William of Normandy led the French-speaking Normans across the English Channel and defeated the English in the Battle of Hastings.[7] As the Normans conquered England, French mingled with Old English, and a new dialect—known today as "Middle English"—emerged.

Three hundred years would pass before anyone attempted to translate the Bible into English again. During that era, church scholars and traveling monks produced plenty of paraphrases and poetic adaptations of the Bible, but it was impossible for anyone who spoke English to read the entire Bible in his or her own language. From the dawn of the English language until the fourteenth century, there was no English translation of the whole Bible, or even of the entire New Testament. In the fourteenth century, a new translation emerged; in time, this English translation would transform the world.

Wessex Gospels

A century after King Alfred the Great translated fifty psalms into English, an unknown scholar translated the four Gospels from Latin into the West Saxon dialect of Old English. These Gospels are known as the Wessex Gospels (c. AD 990). See if you can figure out the first words of the Lord's Prayer in Old English: "Fæder ure þu þe eart on heofonum, si þin nama gehalgod."

Where Did Chapters and Verses Come From?[8]

God didn't inspire the verse or chapter numbers in the Bible. But think about it for a moment: Suppose that you're a teenager and you asked your mother, "Where in the Bible does it say I have to honor you?" Which of the following responses from your mother would make her life easiest?

A. "Go find the Torah scroll. Unroll the scroll a little more than one-third of the way, and find the place where God started giving Moses the Law. Then, you'll need to look about eight inches down the second column and start reading."

B. "Exodus 20:12."

C. "You have questions about whether you need to honor me? Seriously? Go to your room, and stay there until you're hungry enough to figure out who you need to honor!"

The correct answer for making your mother's life easier is, of course, C. But the better answer might be the chapter-and-verse reference in B. The use of numbers to locate verses was made possible by the work of two men whose names you've probably never heard.

- In the early 1200s, Archbishop of Canterbury Stephen Langton added the same chapter numbers to the Latin Vulgate that we still use today.

- While on a trip from Paris to Lyon and back in 1551, Robertus Stephanus (also known as Robert Estienne) divided the chapters into verses in his Greek New Testament. Later, some people joked that he completed this work while riding on his horse, and that each bump in the road had resulted in a new verse number.

- The first English translation to include chapters and verses was the Geneva Bible, published in 1560.

John Wycliffe and the First English Bible

In 1415, a church council gathered in the city of Constance to conduct a heresy trial. The Council of Constance concluded that two Roman Catholic priests had turned into heretics and that both of them must be burned.

Wycliffe giving "the Poor Priests" his translation of the Bible

There was one slight problem with their desire to scorch both priests at the stake: one of the priests was already dead. John Wycliffe had passed away peacefully more than thirty years ago. And so, the bishops did what any sensible church council intent on torching a heretic would do. They decreed that Wycliffe's corpse would be pulled from the grave, burned at the stake, and then pitched into the River Swift. The other priest, Jan Hus, was not quite so fortunate. Hus was still breathing when the executioner lit the branches beneath his feet. (If my fate is to be torched, my preference is to be burned like Wycliffe—a couple of decades after I'm dead. Still, on either side of the grave, being burned at the stake is quite an indignity.)

So what did John Wycliffe do to deserve this fate?

Wycliffe was one of the most brilliant scholars of the fourteenth century, and everyone knew it. When he received his doctoral degree from Oxford University in 1372, he was already recognized as a leading theologian, but his views grew increasingly out of step with the established church.

In time, Wycliffe came to a conclusion that may sound like common sense to us today, but it was a radical claim in the fourteenth century: Scripture, not church tradition, is the final authority in every circumstance and every situation. "Neither the testimony of Augustine nor Jerome nor any other saint should be accepted except insofar as it is based on Scripture," Wycliffe claimed. "Christ's law is best and enough."[9] Since Scripture provides an infallible guide for the Christian life, every Christian—not just the clergy— ought to know the Scriptures. It was this conviction that drove Wycliffe to have the Scriptures translated into English.

"He Made the Bible Common to All … Even to Women!"

In 1374, Wycliffe became a pastor in the English market town of Lutterworth. From here, he sent out "poor preachers" to teach the truths of Scripture in the villages of England. He provided his preachers with sermon outlines and Scripture paraphrases to teach the people—all in English. "Christ and his apostles taught the people in the language best known to them," Wycliffe reasoned. "Therefore, the doctrine should be not only in Latin but also in the [common] tongue."[10]

But Wycliffe wanted to go beyond merely teaching in the common tongue. He became determined that the ordinary people of England should enjoy direct access to the very words of God. And so, he began the process of turning the Latin Vulgate into ordinary English.

Wycliffe didn't actually translate the Bible. Instead, he used his position as a scholar and pastor to have the Bible translated in English. The first edition of the Wycliffe Bible began to circulate in 1382. This edition was little more than a rough word-by-word rendering of the Latin Vulgate into English. Still, for the first time since the dawn of the English language, it was possible to read the entire Bible in English. Smoother English readings followed in later editions.

The men and women who circulated these texts became known as "Lollards." No one knows for certain where the word "Lollard" came from—it probably meant "mumblers" or possibly "weeds"—but it wasn't a compliment. The Lollards didn't hand out Bibles to people, of course. That would have been far too expensive! This was the fourteenth century, and the printing press hadn't yet been invented. Each Wycliffe Bible was copied by hand and cost about six months' wages to produce. Even so, copies of these Bibles circulated widely. Today, more than 600 years later, 176 copies or partial copies of Wycliffe's

New Testament survive; twenty of these are found in complete copies of the Wycliffe Bible.[11]

So what did Lollards do?

They met secretly in small groups known as "cells" and learned the Scriptures in English. A Lollard cell in Buckinghamshire asked a boy to leave their group since they weren't yet certain they could trust him, and then proceeded to recite selections from the Gospels and the letters of Paul. One woman in the Lollard cell at Burford could quote the Ten Commandments in English as well as the epistles of Peter and James in their entirety. But the Lollards did far more than merely meet and memorize! They preached in public places, and they cared for the poor. The truest pilgrimage, one Lollard declared, "is to go barefoot and visit the poor, weak, and sick, for they are the true images of God."[12]

Wycliffe's work was not well-received by church leaders. "Christ gave his Gospel to the clergy and the learned doctors of the Church so that they might give it to the laypeople," one of the church's chroniclers contended. "But this Master John Wycliffe translated the Gospel from Latin into the English. … And Wycliffe, by thus translating the Bible, made it…common to all, … even to women!" The words of the Archbishop of Canterbury were even harsher: "That pestilent and most wretched John Wycliffe, of damnable memory, a child of the old devil, and himself a child or pupil of Antichrist… crowned his wickedness by translating the Scriptures into the mother tongue."[13]

"The Ashes of Wycliffe Are the Emblem of His Doctrine"

Three times, Wycliffe was accused of heresy. Each time, the verdict was derailed before he could be condemned and executed. In 1382, an earthquake rocked the city of London during his hearing, convincing many that God himself had taken Wycliffe's side! The assembly of church leaders convicted Wycliffe anyway, but the favor of the courts and the Parliament kept him from being condemned.

In 1384, Wycliffe suffered a stroke while celebrating the Lord's Supper. He died a few days later, still officially in good standing with his church. Twenty-four years after Wycliffe's death, the Archbishop of Canterbury and an assembly of English bishops forbade any translation of any biblical text "into the English tongue or into any other tongue."[14]

A few years after the Council of Constance condemned Wycliffe in 1415, Wycliffe's body was exhumed and burned. His ashes were dumped into the River Swift which, in the words of a later chronicler, "conveyed his ashes … into the main ocean. And thus the ashes of Wycliffe are the emblem of his doctrine which now is dispersed the world over."[15] A Bohemian priest named Jan Hus was one of those whose thinking was transformed when he read the words of Wycliffe for the first time.

What Happens When You Roast a Lean Goose

Influenced by Wycliffe, Hus freely proclaimed the Scriptures to his people and treated biblical preaching as a mark of the true church, and it was this

sort of preaching that caused the Council of Constance to silence him by burning him alive. According to later legend, Hus—whose name meant "goose"—said to his accusers on the day of his death, "Today you will roast a lean goose, but a hundred years from now you will hear a swan sing, whom you will leave unroasted and no trap or net will catch him for you."[16]

Burning of Jan Hus at the stake

One hundred years later, a German monk rummaging in a library ran across a book of Jan Hus's sermons and asked himself, "For what cause did they burn so great a man? He explained the Scriptures with so much gravity and skill."[17] The German monk's name was Martin Luther. After Luther was declared a heretic and went into hiding in 1521, the first project he undertook was one that would have made Hus and Wycliffe smile: Martin Luther translated the New Testament into German, the language of his people.

Something had, however, happened between the days of Wycliffe and the sixteenth century that made Luther's process of translation far superior to Wycliffe's. What had happened was the publication of a Greek New Testament.

Go West, Greek Manuscripts, Go West!

Wycliffe's Bible had provided English-speaking people with a Bible in their own language, but the Wycliffe Bible suffered from a serious flaw. This translation of the Bible was a translation of a translation. The source that the translators of the Wycliffe Bible used was the Latin Vulgate. Few scholars in medieval Europe knew Greek, and even fewer had attempted to learn Hebrew or Aramaic. And so, even if the translators of the Wycliffe Bible had possessed original-language manuscripts, they couldn't have translated from the Greek New Testament or the Hebrew and Aramaic Old Testament.

"Forasmuch as the Bible contains Christ, that is all that is necessary for salvation, it is necessary for all men, nor for priests alone. It alone is the supreme law that is to rule Church, State, and Christian life, without human traditions and statutes."—John Wycliffe[18]

It was in the fifteenth century that the Greek language worked its way west again. The Muslim Ottomans were conquering the last remnants of the Roman Empire in the East, and many scholars from Greek-speaking regions migrated west into Europe. A renaissance of interest in ancient languages was already in progress in Europe at this time; now, as Greek scholars and manuscripts became available, European universities began offering courses in the Greek language. Meanwhile, Johannes Gutenberg developed the movable metal-type printing press, making mass printing possible for the first time. These new realities set the stage for the publication of the New Testament in Greek.

Johannes Gutenberg developed a movable metal-type press in the 15th century, making possible the mass production of reading materials. The first book that Johannes Gutenberg printed on his printing press was the Latin Vulgate Bible. (Photo courtesy of Dunham Bible Museum, Houston Baptist University)

"I Have Turned My Entire Attention to Greek"

Near the end of the fifteenth century, a young man from the Dutch city of Rotterdam began to learn and to love the Greek language. He was an aspiring scholar, a priest, and the illegitimate son of a priest. By the spring of 1500, his passion for Greek had grown so great that he remarked to a friend, "I have turned my entire attention to Greek. The first thing I shall do, as soon as money arrives, is to buy some Greek authors; after that, I shall buy clothes."[19] The name of this young man who bought Greek before he bought clothes was Desiderius Erasmus of Rotterdam.

Erasmus made it his goal to learn Greek so well that he would be able to use his knowledge of Greek to publish an improved Latin Bible. In 1516, he achieved his goal and, in the process, produced the first published Greek New Testament.[20] Oddly enough, Erasmus' goal in this project wasn't to publish a Greek New Testament at all; his primary purpose was to showcase his fresh rendering of the Latin Bible! He laid the Greek in the left column alongside his Latin translation so readers could see how closely his Latin followed the original text. Prior to this time, the Greek New Testament survived only in hand–copied portions and fragments; now, Bible translators could study the New Testament in its original language in a single mass-printed volume.

In 1516, Erasmus published his *Novum Instrumentum Omne*, a Greek New Testament printed alongside a corrected Latin text. (Photo courtesy of Dunham Bible Museum, Houston Baptist University)

Erasmus only had access to seven or so Greek manuscripts when he developed his New Testament, and the first edition of his Greek New Testament was poorly edited. The second edition was much improved, however, and became the source text for Martin Luther's translation of the New Testament into German. Later editions became the basis for Greek texts published by Robertus Stephanus and edited by Theodore Beza. The third edition of Erasmus's Greek New Testament was perhaps the most important. This third edition was the tool that a man named William Tyndale used to make the New Testament available to the plowboy, the king, and everyone in between.

● ●

Textus Receptus

In 1633, a Greek New Testament published by two brothers named Elzevir included this comment in Latin in the preface: "Textum ergo habes, nunc ab omnibus receptum"—"The text therefore you have, the one now by all received."[21] From the words "textum ... receptum" came the title "Textus Receptus" or "Received Text." The phrase "Textus Receptus" refers to any of the published Greek New Testaments that can be traced back to the text that Erasmus collated in the sixteenth century. This includes important editions published by Robertus Stephanus and edited by Theodore Beza.

● ●

William Tyndale and "the Boy that Driveth the Plow"

You've probably seen the bumper sticker: "If you can read, thank a teacher." Another bumper sticker— or Bible sticker, perhaps—would be every bit as appropriate: "If you can read the Bible in English, thank William Tyndale."

After graduating from Oxford University, William Tyndale began working toward his doctorate in theology, but he became frustrated when he learned that his curriculum didn't include study of the Scriptures. Tyndale's response was to lead his fellow students in Bible studies. He headed to Cambridge University in 1517 and attended there until 1521. By the time he left Cambridge, Tyndale was well on his way to fluency in eight languages.

After leaving Cambridge, Tyndale became a chaplain and children's tutor for a wealthy family. One evening, a visiting priest challenged Tyndale's interpretation of a difficult text. During the debate, the priest declared his perspective on the place of Scripture.

"We had better be without God's law than the pope's," the priest said. In other words, "It would be better to lose God's law than not to have the pope's law."

"If God spares my life," Tyndale retorted, "I will cause a boy that driveth the plow to know more of the Scripture than you do."

> "If God spares my life, I will cause a boy that driveth the plow to know more of the Scripture than you do."—William Tyndale[22]

This goal—to make Scripture accessible to everyone in England—became William Tyndale's driving passion. He requested permission to translate the Greek New Testament into English, but his bishop rejected his request. Tyndale fled to the German provinces and began translating the Scriptures anyway. Unlike any English translator before him, Tyndale worked directly from the Greek and Hebrew texts.

In 1526, Tyndale finished translating the New Testament into English, and a printer in the German city of Worms produced 6,000 copies. The pages for the New Testaments were packaged in watertight boxes inside casks of wine and sacks of flour, smuggled up the Rhine River, and across the North Sea into England. Once the pages arrived in England, they were patched together and sold on the black market.[23]

English bishops bought as many portions of Tyndale's New Testament as they could—sometimes at inflated prices—and burned them. But ecclesiastical pyromaniacs didn't bother Tyndale! "That bishop will burn my New Testament—and I am all the gladder," Tyndale said. "The overplus of the money shall make me more studious to correct the New Testament, and to imprint the same once again." Tyndale did indeed correct his New Testament, and his revision was one of the greatest masterpieces of English prose ever produced. Once the New Testament was finished, Tyndale began translating the Old Testament.

Nearly every English Bible translation throughout the past half-millennium has been influenced somehow by this work from William Tyndale. In fact, without Tyndale's translation of the Bible, the English language itself wouldn't be the same! Tyndale's translations coined dozens of now-common words, like "fisherman," "seashore," and "scapegoat" as well as the modern usage of "beautiful."[24]

But then Tyndale ended up on the wrong side of the king.

A Spanish Cow and an Heir-Less King

Henry VIII, king of England, had offered Tyndale safe passage back to England and a position in the royal court in 1530, but Tyndale refused to return home until the king legalized the publication of the Bible in English. During this time, Henry VIII was seeking a way to swap out his first wife Catherine—whom he called "that Spanish cow"—for Anne Boleyn. The king claimed that, according to Leviticus 20:21, God would never give him an heir through Catherine since she had once been his brother's wife. But the pope refused to revoke the king's wedding vows. After consulting with lawyers in the universities, Henry VIII had the archbishop of Canterbury annul his marriage to Catherine. Then he married Anne, hoping she would bear an heir.

So how did Henry's heir pressures impact the work of William Tyndale?

In 1530, Tyndale published a little tract entitled *Practice of Prelytes.* This tract denounced the annulment of the Henry's wedding vows and landed Tyndale on the list of England's most-wanted outlaws. The next year, King Henry VIII issued an edict declaring "the translation of Scripture corrupted by William Tyndale ... should be utterly expelled, rejected, and put away."[25] Tyndale's translation was one of the greatest masterpieces ever produced in the English language—and yet, one of the many charges brought against him was that he had produced a "corrupted" English Bible!

"Lord, Open the King of England's Eyes!"

One day in 1535, a smooth-talking Englishman named Henry Phillips showed up on Tyndale's doorstep, pretending to support reform in the churches. What Phillips didn't reveal to Tyndale was that he had recently gambled away a small fortune in London. Now, he was surviving on money provided to him to hunt down Tyndale. This gambler clearly didn't know when to hold them, when to fold them, or when to walk away, but he did know how to talk so that people trusted him. He gained Tyndale's trust and then betrayed him into the hands of imperial authorities. For more than a year,

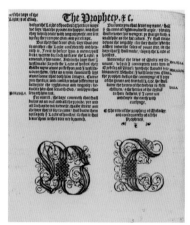

The Matthew's Version was printed with the letters "W T" between the Old and New Testaments, indicating William Tyndale's work as the underlying source. (Photo courtesy of Dunham Bible Museum, Houston Baptist University)

Tyndale suffered in a castle dungeon near Brussels, still determined to finish translating the Old Testament.

One day in the autumn of 1536, Tyndale was taken from his cell and tied to a post. As branches were piled around his feet, he cried out in a loud voice, "Lord! Open the king of England's eyes!"[26] Moments later, he was strangled to death, and his body was set on fire.

The next year, God answered Tyndale's dying plea. King Henry VIII approved the Matthew's Version of the Bible. What the king didn't know was that "Matthew" was a pseudonym. A friend of Tyndale's used the false name "Thomas Matthew" to disguise the fact that this Bible was mostly the work of William Tyndale.[27] The letters "W T" were printed between the Old and New Testaments as a covert tribute to Tyndale's contribution.

Completed and published in 1560, the Geneva Bible was the Bible that the Puritans and Separatists carried with them on the Mayflower in 1620.

Tyndale's Bibles

Coverdale Bible (1535): Myles Coverdale published the first complete English Bible since the publication of the Wycliffe Bible in 1382. The entire New Testament, the first five books of the Old Testament, and probably Jonah were William Tyndale's work. The remainder, Coverdale translated from a variety of sources.

Matthew's Version (1537): John Rogers brought together Tyndale's published and unpublished translations with Coverdale's translation of the Old Testament Prophets (as well as the Apocrypha). This Bible was published under the pseudonym "Thomas Matthew."

Great Bible (1539): Myles Coverdale based this Bible on the Matthew's Version. A copy of the Great Bible was placed in every church in England.

Geneva Bible (1560): The Geneva Bible was used by William Shakespeare and John Bunyan. It was translated by Protestant refugees from England during the reign of Queen Mary I ("Bloody Mary"). Their translation was influenced by the Great Bible and Tyndale's New Testament.

In 1539, King Henry VIII required a copy of the Great Bible—once again, primarily Tyndale's translation—to be purchased by every church in England. And so, two years after Tyndale's martyrdom, God transformed Tyndale's vision into a reality. Even if the boy that drove the plow in England couldn't afford his own Bible, every farm boy could find the Bible in English in his church, and most of the words that the plowboy read in this Bible would be words that came from the hand of William Tyndale.

The Petition from a Thousand Pastors that Birthed a New Bible

In 1603, King James VI of Scotland set out on a journey from Edinburgh to London. Following the death of King Henry VIII, Mary I—Henry's eldest daughter—became queen. She reunited the Church of England with the Roman Catholic Church. After her death, her half-sister Elizabeth took the throne and steered a new course for the Church of England. She tried to find a middle way between Protestantism and Catholicism. Now, Queen Elizabeth I was dead, and her cousin King James VI of Scotland was headed to London to be crowned King James I of England.

King James I

On the way, he was presented with a petition signed by 1,000 Puritan pastors. From the perspective of these pastors, too many Roman Catholic practices still persisted in the Church of England. King James responded by inviting the Puritans to a conference in 1604 at Hampton Court, a sprawling palace of rose-colored brick west of London.

The Puritans' requests ranged from better training for preachers to a shortened liturgy that would eliminate the "longsomeness" of the worship service. When the Puritans suggested that teams of elders ("presbyteries") might lead the church instead of solitary bishops, James took this as an attack on the monarchy

Puritans

Sixteenth- and seventeenth-century English Protestants who regarded the reforms in the Church of England during the reign of Queen Elizabeth I as inadequate.

itself. "If you aim at a presbytery, it agreeth as well with monarchy as God and the devil!" the king retorted, "If there is a presbytery, every Jack and Tom and Will and Dick shall meet and censure me."[28]

There was one particular request, however, that piqued the king's interest. One Puritan leader suggested that perhaps "one only translation of the Bible" should "be authentical and read in church."[29] At this time, two Bibles were widely used in England. The Bishops' Bible was the official Bible, but it was clumsily translated and unpopular. The Geneva Bible, a direct descendant from Tyndale's Bible, was easy-to-read and well-established among the Puritans. However, the study notes in the Geneva Bible made King James nervous. The notes were shaped by the theology of John Calvin and, at times, they seemed to question the absolute power of kings. Such notes were, according to King James, "savoring of dangerous and traitorous conceits."[30]

King James agreed to the idea of a new Bible and called for a translation with no political or theological notes. Forty-seven scholars—some from among the Puritans and some from those who were satisfied with the Church of England as it was—began working on this project. They translated the New Testament primarily from a text that had been adapted from the third edition of Erasmus' Greek New Testament—the same text that Tyndale had used to translate his New Testament.[31]

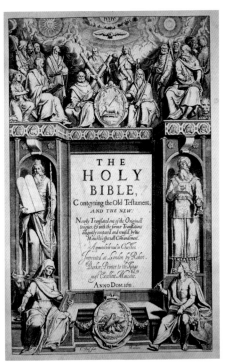

The new translation, published in 1611, became known as "the King James Version" and "the Authorized Version." The title page declared that the Bible had been translated "by his Majesty's special commandment" and was "appointed to be read in churches." By the time they finished their work, the translators had drawn at least two-thirds of the King James Version from translations that could be traced back to William Tyndale.[32] And so, in the King James Version, the words of William Tyndale survive still today.

The King James Version title page, 1611

Timeless Word, Temporary Translations

God's Word is forever and the truths of Scripture are timeless, but every translation of the Bible is temporary.[33] Since language changes over time, every translation eventually reaches an expiration date. At different points in history, the Wycliffe Bible, Tyndale's New Testament, and the Geneva Bible were the finest English translations available. Today, all of these translations—and many more—have passed their point of usefulness.

Between the time of William Tyndale and today, new Greek and Hebrew manuscripts have been discovered, and words have become outdated. Erasmus had only seven medieval Greek manuscripts when he collated his Greek New Testament in the sixteenth century. By the end of the twentieth century, scholars had access to well over 5,000 Greek manuscripts in whole or in part, with some portions dating to the first or second century AD. The result has been a far more accurate reconstruction of the original autographs of Scripture. Furthermore, sixteenth- and seventeenth-century Bibles included terms like "besom" and "wimples" and "crisping pins" that range from confusing to comical today (Isaiah 3:22; 14:23). And don't even get me started on phrases like "my bowels shall sound like an harp" (Isaiah 16:11) that are certain to incite snorts and giggles from middle-schoolers!

In 1870, a team of scholars assembled in Canterbury, England "to adapt King James' version to the present state of the English language" and "to the present standard of biblical scholarship."[34] By this time, the King James Version had already undergone several minor updates, most recently in 1769.[35] Yet, none of these updates had taken into account the growing number of Greek texts that were more ancient than the ones Erasmus had used. This update of the King James Version would work from texts that took into account a wealth of older and more reliable biblical manuscripts.

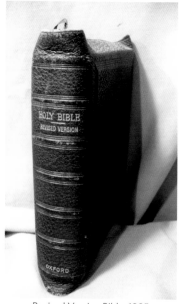

Revised Version Bible, 1885

The new translation that emerged from this team—published in 1885 as the Revised Version in England and in the United States as the American Standard Version in

1901—was the first in a flood of modern English translations. Throughout the twentieth and twenty-first centuries, more discoveries of more biblical manuscripts combined with the growth of more publishers publishing more books and resulted in a surge of new English translations of the Bible.

The pathway to these translations began with a cow-herder singing in the fields of North Yorkshire. The tradition continued with a man who was burned after he was already dead and culminated in William Tyndale's translations that still shape our speech today.

Since Tyndale's time, hundreds more versions of the English Bible have been published. Some versions have been more helpful than others, but nearly all of them have been produced with the same goal that Tyndale declared so many years ago: to provide every person—even "the boy that driveth the plow," in Tyndale's parlance—with an opportunity to read and to understand the Bible. And yet, we do not study the Bible as an end in itself; we read the Bible to know God as he has revealed himself to us in Jesus Christ.[36] As Scripture turns our attention toward the crucified and risen King Jesus, God awakens within us a longing for the salvation and the peace of those around us, knowing that a day is coming soon when "the kingdom of the world [will] become the kingdom of our Lord and of His Christ; and He will reign forever and ever" (Revelation 11:15).

What Makes Different Versions of the Bible So Different?

Have you ever been in a Bible study and wondered, "Why on earth is that person's Bible so different from mine?" Most of the differences between versions of the Bible are because of different perspectives on the best way to translate a text from one language to another. There are three primary approaches when it comes to moving the biblical text from the original languages into a new language:

(1) *Formal equivalence*: A formal equivalent translation of the Bible tries to follow the original Hebrew, Aramaic, and Greek wording as closely as possible. "Formal equivalence focuses attention on the message itself, in both form and content."[37] The New American Standard Bible, the English Standard Version, and the New King James Version are some of the most familiar formal equivalent translations. The strength of a formal equivalent translation is its focus on being faithful to the original text. The weakness of formal equivalent translations is the fact that they tend to be a bit more difficult to read, especially for younger readers or for people who are just learning English.

(2) *Functional (dynamic) equivalence*: A functional equivalent translation usually translates the original languages phrase-by-phrase, following the flow of the biblical text without trying to translate every word. Functional equivalence "aims at complete naturalness of expression" in the English language.[38] The New International Version and the New Living Translation are some of the most familiar functional equivalent translations. The strength of these translations is that they are easy to read, especially for children and new believers. The weakness is that it's difficult to use these translations for any sort of detailed Bible study since so many words and phrases are modified to make the text flow smoothly in English.

(3) *Paraphrase*: A paraphrase really isn't a translation at all. A paraphrase tries to restate the ideas in the biblical text in the ways that we might say them if they were written down today. Paraphrases add a lot of explanations and interpretations along the way. Paraphrases are easy to read, but they aren't meant to follow the exact wording of the original text. The Living Bible and The Message are popular paraphrases.

John 3:16 Across English Translations

Wycliffe (1380s)	For God louede so the world, that he yaf his `oon bigetun sone, that ech man that bileueth in him perische not, but haue euerlastynge lijf.
Tyndale (1525)	For God so loveth the worlde yt he hath geven his only sonne thsat none that beleve in him shuld perisshe: but shuld have everlastinge lyfe.
King James Bible (1611)	For God so loued the world, that he gaue his only begotten Sonne: that whosoeuer beleeueth in him, should not perish, but haue euerlasting life.
Revised Version (1881)	For God so loved the world, that he gave his only begotten Son, that whosoever believeth on him should not perish but have eternal life.
English Standard Version (2001)	For God so loved the world, that he gave his only Son, that whoever believes in him should not perish but have eternal life.
New International Version (2011)	For God so loved the world that he gave his one and only Son, that whoever believes in him shall not perish but have eternal life.

Psalm 23:1–2 Across English Translations

Wycliffe (1380s)	The Lord gouerneth me, and no thing schal faile to me; in the place of pasture there he hath set me. He nurschide me on the watir of refreischyng
King James Bible (1611)	The Lord is my shepheard, I shall not want. He maketh me to lie downe in greene pastures: he leadeth mee beside the still waters.
Revised Version (1881)	The Lord is my shepherd; I shall not want. He maketh me to lie down in green pastures: he leadeth me beside the still waters.
English Standard Version (2001)	The Lord is my shepherd; I shall not want. He makes me lie down in green pastures. He leads me beside still waters.
New International Version (2011)	The Lord is my shepherd, I lack nothing. He makes me lie down in green pastures, he leads me beside quiet waters

A Call to Mission

Billions of English Bibles are available around the globe—but the task of translating Scripture from the original languages is far from finished. Right now, more than 1,800 people-groups do not have a single word of Scripture in a language that they can easily understand. What that means is that unless we translate the Scriptures into these languages, more than 180 million people will live and die without ever having heard God's Word.[39]

Let that sink in for a moment.

More than 180 *million* men, women, and children.

That's six people every second for an entire year.

"The Scriptures … are the fountains of salvation," a fourth-century church leader named Athanasius of Alexandria declared, "so that the one who thirsts may be satisfied with the living words they contain."[40] But, for those who lack the Bible in their language, these living words remain inaccessible.

So what can you do?

You can pray. Ask God specifically to send workers to those who have no access to the Scriptures (Matthew 9:38).

You can give. Find a trustworthy mission agency that translates the Scriptures; contact the agency to find out how you can support translation efforts around the world.

You can go. Could God be calling you to commit your life to translate the Scriptures for unreached people groups? My hope—my prayer—throughout this book has been that God would use the story of how we got the Bible to call men and women to translate the Scriptures. Could it be that one of those people is you?

Appendixes

APPENDIX 1:

Four Perspectives on the Inspiration of Scripture

Perspective	Extent of inspiration	Definition	Evaluation
Illumination	Partial	Inspiration is primarily human. Scripture was written by human authors whose sensitivity to spiritual truths was divinely heightened.	In this view, only the authors wrote the texts. However, according to Paul, God did not merely inspire the authors of Scripture; God inspired Scripture itself (2 Timothy 3:16). This perspective is problematic because it does not adequately take into account the divine aspect of the inspiration of Scripture.
Dynamic Inspiration	Partial or plenary	Inspiration includes both human and divine aspects. God placed concepts in the minds of the authors, and the authors described these concepts using their own words.	In this view, both the authors and the texts were inspired. However, if the Holy Spirit did not superintend the words that the authors chose, it is possible that the inspired authors might have erred when writing Scripture. This perspective could contradict the claims of Jesus that Scripture is completely trustworthy (John 10:35).

Perspective	Extent of inspiration	Definition	Evaluation
Verbal Inspiration	Plenary	Inspiration includes both human and divine aspects. God placed concepts in the minds of the authors, and God guided the authors so that they never erred in the words that they chose.	In this view, both the authors and the texts were inspired. Scripture is God-breathed and free from error because the guidance of the Holy Spirit extends beyond the implanting of ideas to the choice of words. Verbal inspiration is a truth that Christians have confessed for centuries regarding Scripture.
Dictation	Plenary	Inspiration is primarily divine. God dictated every part of Scripture word-by-word to the authors.	In this view, the texts were inspired, and the authors recorded words that the Holy Spirit dictated. However, if God dictated every word without regard for the will of the individual author, it is difficult to explain how different biblical authors wrote in such distinct and identifiable styles. This perspective is problematic because it does not adequately take into account the human aspect of the inspiration of Scripture.

(Plenary = "full," every part)

APPENDIX 2:

Four Views of the Nature of Scripture

View	Description
Scripture is Inerrant and Infallible Revelation	The Bible is God-breathed and error-free. Scripture is true in everything it affirms, not only in what it says about spiritual truths but also when it addresses history and science. The Bible never errs and never fails to accomplish God's saving and sanctifying purposes.
Scripture is Infallible Revelation	In some contexts, infallible has carried a meaning equal to or stronger than "inerrancy." The Bible is not merely inerrant but also unable to err. Since the 1970s, however, infallibility has also been used at times to mean that the Bible never fails to accomplish God's saving purposes but that the Bible may contain errors related to other areas, including history and science.
Scripture is Authoritative and Normative Revelation	Those who affirm that Scripture is inerrant or infallible would also affirm that Scripture is authoritative and normative for God's people. Some theologians are, however, uncomfortable with the term "inerrancy." For many of them, "inerrancy" is seen as a recent, uniquely American innovation. Some theologians who reject the word "inerrancy" and prefer terms such as authoritative and normative argue that the question of whether or not the Bible might contain occasional errors or misstatements is irrelevant; the Bible is meant to guide God's people and to serve as a narrative of God's saving power. The possibility of scientific or historical misstatements does not prevent the Bible from serving as God's authoritative and normative revelation for his people.
Scripture is an Errant Record of Religious Experience	The Bible is merely a collection of human religious reflections and likely contains numerous errors. For some who view the Bible in this way, the words of Scripture have meaning but are devoid of divine authority. For others, the Bible is only God's Word in the sense that God chooses uniquely to speak through it to his people. God's revelation is not found in the meaning of the biblical text but in what the Holy Spirit is revealing to his people as they read the text and encounter God through this revelatory event.

Appendix **3:**

Did Moses *really* write the Torah?

Before the modern era, nearly every biblical scholar assumed that most of the Torah could be traced back to Moses. It wasn't until the seventeenth century that skeptics began to question how much Moses really had to do with the Torah. By the nineteenth century, many critical scholars had concluded that Moses had little (if anything) to do with the Torah and that the sources behind the Torah were written long after Moses was dead.

A German scholar named Julius Wellhausen proposed a sequence and structure for these sources that became known as "the documentary hypothesis." The documentary hypothesis assumed that Israel's faith evolved over a half-millennium from a primitive tribal religion into a sophisticated ritual religion. Here are the sources and sequence that Wellhausen proposed:

Source	Date	Description
J (Jahwist) Source	10th century BC	Parts of Genesis, Exodus, and Numbers; written in Judah almost 500 years after Moses. Primarily described God using the Hebrew name "YHWH" ("Jawheh" in German, translated in most English Bibles as "the Lord").
E (Elohist) Source	9th century BC	Parts of Genesis, Exodus, and Numbers; written in Israel. Primarily described God using the Hebrew title "Elohim" (translated in English Bibles as "God").
D (Deuteronomic) Source	7th, 6th, and 5th centuries BC	Deuteronomy (as well as Joshua, Judges, 1 and 2 Samuel, 1 and 2 Kings); began to develop in Judah. Hilkiah the priest did not *find* the book of Deuteronomy in the temple as he claimed (2 Kings 22:8); instead, Deuteronomy was *forged* during this era for the purpose of furthering King Josiah's reforms.[1]
P (Priestly) Source	6th and 5th centuries BC	Parts of Genesis, Exodus, and Numbers, all of Leviticus; shaped during and after the exile. Focused on covenants, rituals, and genealogies.

It's true that the Torah pulls together multiple sources, and some of these segments *do* seem to have been added after the time of Moses. Here are a few examples of possible post-Moses editing:

✣ "Now the man Moses was very meek," we read in the Torah, "more than all the people who were on the face of the earth" (Numbers 12:3). Later in the Torah, we find these words: "There has not arisen a prophet since in Israel like Moses" (Deuteronomy 34:10). It's possible that words like these may have been written by someone other than Moses.

✣ Locations are sometimes described using a name or a form that emerged later. The city of Dan, for example, wasn't called "Dan" until the days of the judges (Genesis 14:14; Judges 18:29).

✣ The final chapter of Deuteronomy describes the death and burial of Moses (34:5–8). Even for the greatest and meekest prophet in Israel's history, writing from beyond the grave seems like a bit of a stretch!

And so, later prophets and scribes *do* seem to have shaped certain segments of the Torah. Still, that doesn't mean we must accept a documentary hypothesis that places the creation of the Torah centuries after Moses died. In fact, recent scholarship has repeatedly demonstrated that, despite its popularity, the documentary hypothesis can't adequately explain Israel's history. Evidences from history and archaeology continue to support the possibility that Moses wrote the texts that were turned into the Torah. "The documentary hypothesis is a zombie," Old Testament scholar Duane Garrett has written, "it is dead but still roaming the halls of Old Testament scholarship seeking its next victim."[2]

Here are a few facts that may be helpful if you're wondering whether Moses could really have written the Torah:

✣ Some skeptics have claimed that no one in Moses' context could have composed literature like the Torah—but archaeological discoveries reveal that a wide range of literary documents were in fact being written during the time of Moses. About fifty miles from Mount Sinai, inscriptions from the time of Moses have been discovered, etched in stone in an alphabetic script. Scribes in regions ranging from Sinai to Canaan were clearly capable of producing literary documents during Moses' lifetime. If Moses was educated in the courts of an Egyptian Pharaoh, it is entirely conceivable that he had access to scribal training.[3]

✢ The use of different names for God in certain texts does not mean these texts come from different time-periods. It seems that the name "YHWH" ("the Lord") was connected to God's covenant with Israel while the title "Elohim" ("God") emphasized God's sovereignty over all the earth. Moses could have used earlier sources that focused on specific aspects of God's character, or Moses himself may have chosen these emphases.

✢ Some sections of Torah explicitly identify Moses as the author (Exodus 24:4; Deuteronomy 31:9–24).

✢ Jesus identified Moses as the author of Torah (Matthew 8:4; Mark 7:10; 12:26).

The Old Testament was a time of continuing revelation from God. If later inspired scribes wove sources together in the Torah or later prophets clarified names and places, it does not mean that they corrupted the text. Instead, God superintended not only the creation of the sources but also their collection and organization. The result of this process is that every clause was precisely the one that God intended. As Duane Garrett notes, "The assertion that Moses is the principal author of the present text of Genesis need not mean that it came from his hand exactly as we have it now. ... The main reason such [redactions] would have taken place was not to substantially change the book ... but rather to make it more intelligible for a later generation of readers."[4]

APPENDIX 4:

The Lost Gospels

Here's a summary of many of the lost Gospels, nearly all of which were written too late to have come from eyewitnesses:

Lost Gospel	Origin/Date	Description
Gospel of Basilides	Gnostic writing, mid-2nd century AD	Gnostic writing, now lost, mentioned by several early Christians.
Gospel of the Ebionites	Ebionite writing, 2nd century AD	Surviving only in fragmented quotations in the writings of early Christians, *Gospel of the Ebionites* may have been a variation of *Gospel of the Hebrews*, edited to fit the theology of a sect known as "Ebionites." The Ebionites believed that Jesus was a human being, adopted by God at his baptism.
Egerton Gospel	Fragments from an ancient document, 2nd century AD	Not actually a Gospel but a few fragments from an unknown source, the "Egerton Gospel" includes four stories about Jesus. Three of these stories appear, in varying forms, in the New Testament Gospels (Mark 1:40–45; 12:13–17; John 5:39–47; 10:33–39).
Gospel of the Egyptians	Ancient writing, perhaps Gnostic, 2nd century AD	Presented as a dialogue between Jesus and a female disciple named Salome, *Gospel of the Egyptians* encourages all believers to practice celibacy.
Coptic Gospel of the Egyptians	Gnostic writing, late 3rd century AD	Coptic Gospel of the Egyptians recounts a Gnostic myth in which Jesus is presented as a reincarnation of Seth, the third son of Adam and Eve.

Lost Gospel	Origin/Date	Description
Gospel of Eve	Gnostic writing, probably 3rd century AD	Lost Gnostic writing, quoted by Epiphanius of Salamis. *Gospel of Eve* was written at least a century after the time of Jesus. Perhaps also known as *Gospel of Perfection*.
Gospel of the Hebrews	Christian writing, 1st or 2nd century AD	*Gospel of the Hebrews* survives only in quotations found in the writings of early Christians. Some scholars believe *Gospel of the Hebrews* represents an Aramaic summary of Jesus' life. Also known as *Gospel of the Nazoreans*.
Infancy Gospel of James	Christian writing, late 2nd century AD	An account, supposedly written by James, of the life of Mary. According to this document, Mary the mother of Jesus remained a virgin throughout her life.
Gospel of Jesus' Wife	Modern forgery	Not a Gospel but a forged fragment which includes the words in Coptic, "Jesus said to them, 'My wife.'" Although the papyrus is ancient, the writing on the papyrus is not. The same individual who forged this fragment seems to have produced a forged portion of John's Gospel that copied an authentic 5th-century text known as Codex Qau.
Acts of John	Docetic writing, late 2nd century AD	Supposed retelling of events from the life of the apostle John. Some copies of this text include comments that are Docetic—that is, they imply that Jesus Christ was not fully human—but these comments are not present in every version. It is possible that they were added later.

Lost Gospel	Origin/Date	Description
Gospel of Judas	Gnostic writing, late 2nd century AD	Supposed account of the life of Jesus in which Judas Iscariot is portrayed as a heroic figure, commanded by Jesus to act as the betrayer.
Gospel of the Lord	Marcionite writing, mid-2nd century AD	Alteration of the Gospel According to Luke, edited to fit Marcion's theology.
Gospel of Mary	Gnostic writing, late 2nd century AD	Although frequently called *Gospel of Mary Magdalene*, the text of this document never indicates which biblical Mary is the story's central character.
Gospel of Matthias	Ancient writing, perhaps Gnostic, 2nd century AD	Lost document.
Gospel of Nicodemus	Forgery, 4th century AD	Forgery that sometimes circulated as part of *Acts of Pilate*, also a late and spurious account.
Oxyrhynchus Gospel	Christian writing, 2nd century AD	Not actually a Gospel but a tiny papyrus fragment from an unknown source, the "Oxyrhynchus Gospel" describes a confrontation between Jesus and the Pharisees. The events described in this fragment do not contradict any New Testament Gospels and seem to represent an expansion or alternative version of the events described in Mark 7:1–23.

Lost Gospel	Origin/Date	Description
Gospel of Peter	Christian writing, 2nd century AD	Although familiar to many early Christians, this text was not received as an authoritative account of the life of Jesus because (1) it could not be clearly connected to the apostle Peter and (2) some passages in the book could be construed to suggest that Jesus wasn't fully human.
Apocalypse of Peter	Christian writing, 2nd century AD	An apocalyptic text that seems to have circulated with *Gospel of Peter*, *Apocalypse of Peter* seems to have been written in the early to mid-2nd century, 70 years or so after the death of the apostle Peter.
Coptic Apocalypse of Peter	Gnostic writing, late 3rd century AD	*The Coptic Apocalypse of Peter* clearly denied that Jesus had a physical body, declaring that "the one whose hands and feet they nailed to the cross [was] only a fleshly substitute."
Gospel of Philip	Gnostic writing, 3rd century AD	Not actually a Gospel but a collection of brief excerpts from other Gnostic writings, *Gospel of Philip* summarizes the views of the followers of the Gnostic leader Valentinus.
Q	Hypothetical source	Not actually a Gospel at all, or even a surviving document, but a hypothetical collection of sayings that appear in both Matthew's and Luke's Gospels. Approximately 230 sayings in the New Testament Gospels have been identified as part of this hypothetical source.

Lost Gospel	Origin/Date	Description
Gospel of the Savior	Gnostic writing, early 3rd century AD	Not actually a Gospel but a few fragments from an ancient document known as Papyrus Berlin 22220, *Gospel of the Savior* seems to have been a Gnostic adaptation of *Gospel of Peter*. Also known as *Vision of the Savior*.
Gospel of Thomas	Gnostic writing, mid-2nd century AD	Not actually a Gospel, but a collection of sayings attributed to Jesus. Most sayings in *Gospel of Thomas* are similar to statements found in the New Testament Gospels. A few, however, seem to represent early Gnostic trends. Although some sayings in the book can be traced to the 1st century AD, the book probably did not emerge in its surviving form until the middle of the 2nd century.
Infancy Gospel of Thomas	Christian writing, late 2nd century AD	An account of the childhood of Jesus, supposedly written by the apostle Thomas. In this text, the boy Jesus uses his miraculous powers for his own benefit. The author's style of writing and his lack of knowledge about Jewish traditions suggest that the book was written in the late 2nd century AD, long after the death of the apostle Thomas.
Gospel of Truth	Gnostic writing, late 2nd century AD	Unearthed at Nag Hammadi in the 1940s, *Gospel of Truth* is a Gnostic retelling of the creation story and of the life of Jesus. According to Irenaeus of Lyons, a disciple of a Gnostic teacher named Valentinus wrote *Gospel of Truth*, also known as *Gospel of Valentinus*.

APPENDIX 5:

English Bible Translations Comparison

Translation	Year*	Type	Description
King James Version (KJV)	1611, 1769	Formal Equivalent	In 1604, King James I of England authorized a new translation of the Bible.
American Standard Version (ASV)	1901	Formal Equivalent	American edition of English Revised Version, a late 19th-century revision of the KJV.
Revised Standard Version (RSV)	1952	Formal Equivalent	Based on the ASV.
Amplified Bible (AMP)	1965	Formal Equivalent, plus amplification of meaning	Attempts to express the original text through the use of explanatory alternate readings and amplifications.
New Jerusalem Bible (NJB)	1966, 1985	Formal Equivalent	Typically used by Roman Catholics for serious Bible study. Includes the Apocrypha.
New American Bible (NAB)	1970, 1986, 1991	Formal Equivalent	Official translation used in U.S. Catholic Church Mass. Includes the Apocrypha.
New American Standard Bible (NASB)	1971, 1995	Formal Equivalent	Attempts to render grammar and terminology in clear English while preserving literal accuracy of ASV.
Good News Translation (GNT)	1976, 1992	Functional Equivalent	A "common language" Bible, also known as Today's English Version.

Translation	Year*	Type	Description
New International Version (NIV)	1978, 1984, 2011	Translation approach varies	Tries to bring modern Bible readers as close as possible to the experience of the first Bible readers.
New King James Version (NKJV)	1982	Formal Equivalent	Modern translation intended to maintain stylistic beauty of the KJV. New Testament translated from a reconstruction of Greek text used by the King James Version translators.
New Century Version (NCV)	1987	Functional Equivalent	English translation derived from English Version for the Deaf (EVD) and the Easy-to-Read Version (ERV).
New Revised Standard Version (NRSV)	1989	Formal Equivalent	Revision of RSV intended to be "as literal as possible" and "as free as necessary."
Contemporary English Version (CEV)	1995	Functional Equivalent	Intended to be easily read by grade-schoolers and second language readers.
God's Word Translation (GW)	1995	Natural Equivalent	Translated by a committee of biblical scholars and English reviewers to ensure accurate, natural English.
New International Reader's Version (NIrV)	1996, 1998	Functional Equivalent	Based on the NIV, with simpler words and shorter sentences.
New Living Translation (NLT)	1996, 2004	Functional Equivalent	Attempts to translate entire thoughts (rather than just words) into natural, everyday English.

Translation	Year*	Type	Description
English Standard Version (ESV)	2001	Formal Equivalent	Essentially literal, based on the 1971 RSV with significant corrections and language updates.
The Message (MSG)	2002	Paraphrase	Strives to capture idiomatic flavor of original texts to engage people in the reading process.
Holman Christian Standard Bible (HCSB)	2004	Optimal Equivalent	Pursued two ideals: each word must reflect contemporary English and each word must be faithful to the original languages.
Common English Bible (CEB)	2011	Translation approach varies	Attempts to substitute more natural wordings for traditional biblical terminology.

*Year complete Bible translation was released and later revisions

Formal Equivalent: Translation of the Bible that tries to follow the original Hebrew, Aramaic, and Greek wording as closely as possible.

Functional (Dynamic) Equivalent: Usually translates the original languages phrase-by-phrase, following the flow of the biblical text without trying to translate every word.

Optimal (Natural) Equivalent: Between a word-for-word and thought-for-thought approach.

Paraphrase: Tries to restate the ideas in the biblical text in the ways that we might say them if they were written down today.

Acknowledgements

My interest in how we got the Bible began when I couldn't find the Textus Receptus.

I grew up in a succession of churches where the King James Version was seen as the sole reliable rendering of the Scriptures. The primary enemies of Christian faith in these congregations were rock music, Russian communists, and every translation of the Bible other than the King James Version—or at least that's how it seemed to me as a teenager.

By the time I started college, the Berlin Wall had been in shambles for nearly a year; so, Russia didn't seem like much of a menace anymore. Petra and Stryper—the two primary bands in my cassette collection—probably used enough hair spray to threaten the global supply of Aqua Net®, but their brand of rock music posed little threat to my faith. I remained quite convinced, however, that every translation other than the King James Version represented a seething cesspool of heresy.

According to what I'd been taught, the Word of God had been perfectly preserved with no variants for nearly two thousand years in a mystical manuscript known as "the Received Text"—or "Textus Receptus" in Latin. The translators of the King James Version had worked from this perfect text when they translated the Bible—or so I'd been told. Sometime in the nineteenth century, liberal scholars began using corrupted manuscripts to prop up their attempts to change the Bible. Every translation completed after 1611 was a product of this liberal assault on the Scriptures.

When I started learning about Greek and Hebrew and the origins of the Bible in college, I wanted to defend the perfectly-preserved Scriptures. And so, I decided to learn more about the Textus Receptus. One of the first tasks I undertook was to determine where the Textus Receptus was kept today. Once I began looking for this manuscript, many of my assumptions about the Scriptures began to crumble.

What I found out first was that the Textus Receptus wasn't an ancient manuscript at all. The phrase "Textus Receptus" referred to an entire succession of printed Greek New Testaments that could be traced back to a text published in 1516 by a Roman Catholic priest named Erasmus—and not one of these editions agreed word-for-word with the others. What's more, the translators of the King James Version worked from at least a couple of different New Testaments—Theodore Beza's 1598 New Testament and a 1550 edition from Robertus Stephanus—and these two Greek texts weren't completely identical either. Even more disturbing was the fact that the phrase "Textus Receptus" hadn't even been applied to this family of Greek New Testaments until 1633—twenty-two years after the King James Version was published. In short, everything I'd been told about the origins of the New Testament turned out to be untrue.

It took me several months to wrestle through these challenges and several others that emerged alongside them. In the end, I left behind my trust in the supremacy of one single version of the Bible—but I ended up believing more than ever before in the truths that the Bible taught. I never did find that one fabled manuscript that preserved every syllable of Scripture without a single variant. What I found instead were thousands of manuscripts that, taken together, have preserved the Word of God sufficiently for us to trust and to follow Jesus Christ.

What I've worked to develop in *How We Got the Bible* is the type of book that I needed back then as I struggled to understand the origins of Scripture. My hope has been to produce a book that was honest about the many difficulties in the biblical manuscripts. Yet I also wanted readers to understand why these differences should never distract us from total trust in the inspiration and inerrancy of the Scriptures.

The words that you read in these pages have been sharpened through invaluable critiques and comments from my assistants Garrick Bailey and Nick Weyrens; my esteemed colleagues Rob Plummer, Jonathan Pennington, and Gregg Allison; Southern Seminary doctoral students Aubrey Sequeira and Andrew King; and, layperson Bill Bensinger. This book was fueled by caffeinated potables consumed at the Starbucks on Frankfort Avenue in Louisville and at the single finest coffee shop in the cosmos, Quills on Baxter Avenue.

Seventeen years ago, Carol Witte and Gretchen Goldsmith at Rose Publishing took a chance on an unsolicited manuscript from an unknown pastor of a tiny church in rural Missouri. That manuscript became *Christian History Made Easy* and marked the beginning of my career as a writer. I remain thankful for my many fellow-laborers at Rose Publishing, particularly two long-suffering editors Lynnette Pennings and Jessica Curiel.

I continue to be thankful for the privilege of serving on the faculty of The Southern Baptist Theological Seminary. Provost Randy Stinson and Dean Adam Greenway consistently create a culture that supports the writing efforts of faculty. Generous book allowances from trustees and an outstanding library staff at Boyce Centennial Library guarantee that faculty never lack research resources.

Greatest of all, I am grateful to the God who has enlivened me to the wonders of his grace; second only to my gratitude for God's grace, I am grateful for the wife and three daughters through whom God floods my life with undeserved joy and sustaining grace. This book is dedicated to my wife Rayann; more thanks are due to her than mere words could ever express. Without her constant encouragement and support over the past two decades, nothing that I have written would ever have been possible. There has never been a moment when I have felt anything less than eager anticipation when I return home at night. In this way and in so many others, I am supremely blessed.

Notes

Chapter 1

1. The initial draft of this chapter was researched and written by Derek Brown.

2. There is evidence in the Bible that God may at times guide an individual to speak a greater message than he or she intends. For example, in John 11:47–52, Caiaphas declared that Jesus should die in place of the people, intending that the death of Jesus would keep the Romans from destroying the temple and the people; however, what God revealed through his words was that Jesus would bring Jews and Gentiles together by dying for the sins both of Jews and Gentiles. See S. Lewis Johnson, *The Old Testament in the New* (Grand Rapids: Zondervan, 1980), 94.

3. See Paul D. Wegner, *The Journey from Text to Translation: The Origin and Development of the Bible* (Grand Rapids: BakerAcademic, 1999), 30-31; Norman L. Geisler and William E. Nix, *A General Introduction to the Bible*, Revised and Expanded (Chicago: Moody, 1986), 21–22.

4. Wegner, *The Journey from Text to Translation*, 30.

5. Wegner, *The Journey from Text to Translation*, 30. Wegner notes that the Septuagint—a Greek translation of the Old Testament written sometime between 250 and 100 BC— uses the word *biblia* in Daniel 9:2 "to refer to Jeremiah's words, which may have been in the form of letters or a collection of prophets."

6. Tertullian, *Against Praxeas*, 15; Tertullian, *Against Marcion*, 3:14; 4:6.

7. C. S. Lewis, *The Voyage of the Dawn Treader* (*London: Bless, 1952*), 159.

8. B. B. Warfield wrote extensively defending the idea that *theopneustos* means "God-breathed." See *The Inspiration and Authority of the Bible* (Reprint; Philadelphia: Presbyterian and Reformed, 1948).

9. For more on Jesus' view of the Old Testament, see John Wenham, *Christ and the Bible* (Downers Grove, IL: InterVarsity, 1973), 11-37.

10. While usage of the word "inerrancy" to describe the nature of Scripture is recent, the concept of an error-free Bible has been affirmed throughout the history of the church. For a helpful historical survey from the early church forward, see Tom Nettles, "Inerrancy in History," in *Authority and Interpretation*, ed. Duane Garrett and Richard Melik (Grand Rapids: Baker, 1987), 127–54.

11. The English word "inerrancy" was not commonly used until the last half of the nineteenth century. The earliest usages of the word seem to have been in critical descriptions of the powers of the Roman Catholic pope. Near the end of the nineteenth century, an opponent of the total truthfulness of Scripture—Presbyterian pastor Charles Augustus Briggs—took up the term to describe the view of Scripture that he rejected

(see C. A. Briggs, *Inspiration and Inerrancy* [London: Clarke, 1891]). Throughout the twentieth century, the term inerrancy grew in popularity among conservative evangelical and fundamentalist Christians. Due in part to distortions and dilutions of the term "infallibility" in the latter part of the twentieth century, it became necessary to elevate the importance of concept of inerrancy and to articulate more clearly the meaning of the term. In 1978, more than three hundred evangelical leaders gathered to form the International Council on Biblical Inerrancy. Over the span of eight years, this council developed three documents that articulated the meaning and implications of biblical inerrancy: "The Chicago Statement on Biblical Inerrancy" (1978), "The Chicago Statement on Biblical Hermeneutics" (1982), and "The Chicago Statement on Biblical Application" (1986).

12. Paul D. Feinberg, "The Meaning of Inerrancy," in *Inerrancy* ed. by Norman Geisler (Grand Rapids: Zondervan, 1980), 294. It has been argued in recent decades that God never intended to give accurate information about historical, geographic, or scientific matters in Scripture, but only to provide his people with truth about the way of salvation and issues pertaining to Christian living. This argument fails for two reasons. (1) It is impossible to separate such pronouncements of Scripture from matters related to salvation and Christian living. What we believe about God and Jesus Christ is grounded in and so intertwined with history and with the reliability of other biblical pronouncements that to discount one is to remove our grounds for confidence in the other. (2) Such a position disregards what the church has always believed about the Bible: that it is wholly true and without error in everything it affirms. For more on the church's historical position on the trustworthiness of Scripture, see John Woodbridge, *Biblical Authority* (Grand Rapids: Zondervan, 1982), and, John Hannah, ed., *Inerrancy and the Church* (Chicago: Moody, 1984).

13. Chicago Statement on Biblical Inerrancy, Exposition: Infallibility, Inerrancy, Interpretation.

14. Article 13 of The Chicago Statement on Biblical Inerrancy helpfully clarifies the meaning of inerrancy in relation to issues such as round numbers, figurative languages, and similar features of the biblical text. "We affirm the propriety of using inerrancy as a theological term with reference to the complete truthfulness of Scripture. We deny that it is proper to evaluate Scripture according to standards of truth and error that are alien to its usage or purpose. We further deny that inerrancy is negated by biblical phenomena such as a lack of modern technical precision, irregularities of grammar or spelling, observational descriptions of nature, the reporting of falsehoods, the use of hyperbole and round numbers, the topical arrangement of material, variant selections of material in parallel accounts, or the use of free citations."

15. John Frame, *The Doctrine of the Word of God*, vol. 4 of *A Theology of Lordship* (Phillipsburg, NJ: P & R, 2010), 173.

16. Clement of Rome, *Letter to the Corinthians*, 45.

17. Irenaeus, *Against Heresies*, 2:28:3.

18. Justin Martyr, *Dialogue with Trypho*, 65.

19. Tertullian of Carthage, *Treatise on the Soul*, 21.

20. Athanasius of Alexandria, *Easter Letter,* 19:3.

21. Augustine of Hippo, *Letters*, 82.

22. Wayne Grudem, *Systematic Theology* (Kindle edition; Grand Rapids: Zondervan, 1994), 129.

23. Chicago Statement on Biblical Inerrancy, articles 1, 11, and 12.

24. Greg L. Bahnsen, "The Inerrancy of the Autographa," in *Inerrancy*, ed. by Norman Geisler, 151–193.

25. For more information on the practice of textual criticism and the reliability of the biblical texts, see Daniel Wallace, "The Reliability of the New Testament Manuscripts," in *Understanding Scripture*, ed. Wayne Grudem, C. John Collins, and Thomas R. Schreiner (Wheaton, IL: Crossway, 2012), and, Timothy Paul Jones, *Misquoting Truth* (Downer's Grove, IL: IVP, 2007).

26. David Prince, "The Necessity of a Christocentric Kingdom-Focused Model of Expository Preaching" (Ph.D. dissertation, The Southern Baptist Theological Seminary, 2011), 29.

27. R. Albert Mohler, *He is Not Silent* (Chicago: Moody, 2008), 96.

28. John Calvin, *Institutio Christianae Religionis*, 3:2:32.

29. Jerome, Preface to Eustochium, *Commentarii in Isaiam.*

30. N. T. Wright, *Surprised by Scripture* (New York: HarperOne, 2014), 28.

31. Timothy Ward, *Words of Life* (Downers Grove, IL: InterVarsity, 2009), 52–56.

How We Got the Old Testament

1. Peter Gentry and Stephen Wellum, *Kingdom through Covenant* (Wheaton: Crossway, 2012), 100–101.

2. Tertullian of Carthage, *Adversus Marcionem*, 1.

Chapter 2

1. Terence Noble, ed., "Introduction," Wycliffe's Bible (Kindle edition) 2012.

2. Scot McKnight, *The King Jesus Gospel* (Grand Rapids: Zondervan, 2011), 50, 118.

3. This definition has been shaped by Peter Gentry and Stephen Wellum, *Kingdom through Covenant* (Wheaton: Crossway, 2013) chapter 4; Gordon Hugenberger, *Marriage as Covenant* (Leiden: Brill, 1994); Daniel Lane, "The Meaning and Use of the Old Testament Term for 'Covenant'" (Ph.D. diss., Trinity International University, 2000).

4. For one of the earliest references to the Christian Scriptures as the "New Testament," see Tertullian of Carthage, *Adversus Marcionem*, 4:6.

5. Samuel Emadi wrote an early draft of this chapter and contributed much of the research.

6. The glory of God was removed from the temple prior to the destruction of Jerusalem in 586 BC (Ezekiel 8:6–10:18) suggesting perhaps that articles such as the ark of the covenant could now be touched and taken by other nations. According to Chronicles, every article from the temple was removed and taken to Babylon (2 Chronicles 36:18); however, the ark is not listed when the articles are returned (Ezra 1:7–11). This omission might suggest either that the ark was lost between the removal and the return (for this assumption, see apocryphal text 4 Ezra 10:19–22) or that the ark was hidden prior to the Babylonian invasion (for this possibility, see apocryphal text 2 Maccabees 2:4–10).

7. See Irenaeus of Lyons, *Adversus Haereses*, 3:21:2. For defense of the notion that the Psalms in particular were intentionally ordered by a later editor, see Robert Cole, *Psalms 1-2: Gateway to the Psalter*, Hebrew Bible Monographs 37 (Sheffield: Sheffield Phoenix Press, 2012).

8. Paul Wegner, *The Journey From Texts to Translations* (Grand Rapids: Baker, 2004), 42.

9. This section draws extensively from Ernst Wörthwein with A.A. Fischer, *The Text of the Old Testament* third edition (Grand Rapids: Eerdmans, 2014).

10. Pliny, *Natural History*, 13:74–82.

11. "Hear, O Israel: The LORD our God, the LORD is one" (Deuteronomy 6:4 English Standard Version).

12. Bruce Waltke, "Old Testament Textual Criticism," *Foundations for Biblical Interpretation*, ed. David Dockery, et al. (Nashville: Broadman and Holman, 1994), 175.

13. Neil Lightfoot, *How We Got the Bible* third edition (Grand Rapids: Baker, 2003), 130–131; Wegner, *The Journey From Texts to Translations*, 165–166.

14. Four successive groups of scribes seem to have preserved the Old Testament: (1) Prior to the second century AD, the *Sopherim*—so called because they counted (Hebrew, *saphar*) every letter—copied the Old Testament, followed by (2) the *Tannaim* (second century AD through third century AD) and (3) the *Amoraim* (fourth century AD though fifth century AD). (4) The Masoretes emerged near the end of the fifth century AD. The two major Masoretic clans were Ben Asher and Ben Naphtali. Their texts did differ but not significantly. See Paul Wegner, *A Student's Guide to Textual Criticism of the Bible* (Downers Grove: InterVarsity, 2006), 63–78.

15. Wegner, *The Journey From Texts to Translations*, 172–177.

16. Bill Arnold and Bryan Beyer, *Encountering the Old Testament* (Grand Rapids: Baker, 1999), 26–28.

17. Some scholars have estimated that the agreement among Old Testament manuscripts exceeds ninety percent. See W. W. Klein, Craig Blomberg, and Robert Hubbard, *Introduction to Biblical Interpretation* rev. ed. (Nashville: Nelson, 2004), 122.

18. For references related to the Nash Papyrus, see Wegner, *A Student's Guide to Textual Criticism of the Bible*, 148–151. In 1985, two seventh-century silver amulets were discovered with portions of Numbers 6:22–27 written on them.

19. Frederic Kenyon, *Our Bible and the Ancient Manuscripts* rev. ed. (New York: Harper, 1958), 34–35, 78–79.

20. 1QS, 7; 4Q258. There were, of course, understandable reasons for each of these strictures in the cultural context of the Qumran community.

Chapter 3

1. Samuel Emadi wrote an early draft of this chapter and contributed much of the research.

2. 1 Maccabees 9:27.

3. Roman Catholic theologians tend to treat "deuterocanonical" as a chronological classification, meaning simply that these texts were recognized as canonical at a later time than other Old Testament texts. The Orthodox Church sees the term as a canonical classification, asserting that these books belong in the Bible and are worthy to be read (*Anagignoskomena*) but that their authority is secondary to the rest of Scripture.

4. Jerome, *Incipit Prologus Sancti Hieronymi in Libro Regum,* in *Biblia Sacra Vulgata*; see also Jerome's letter to Paulinus, *Epistula* 53. For further exploration of this topic, see Roger T. Beckwith, "The Apocrypha," in *Understanding Scripture*, ed. Wayne Grudem, C. John Collins, and Thomas R. Schreiner (Wheaton: Crossway, 2012), 90–91.

5. Augustine of Hippo, *De Civitate Dei,* 18:43-44.

6. For further information on definition and development of *kanon*, see H. W. Beyer, "*kanon*," in *Theological Dictionary of the New Testament* vol. 3, ed. Gerhard Kittel, trans. Geoffrey Bromiley (Grand Rapids: Eerdmans, 1966), 597.

7. Paul Wegner, *The Journey From Texts to Translations* (Grand Rapids: Baker, 2004), 101–102.

8. Bill Warren and Archie W. England, "Bible Formation and Canon," *Holman Illustrated Bible Dictionary*, ed. Charles Draper, et al. www.mystudybible.com.

9. 1 Maccabees 4:46; 9:27; 14:41.

10. Several aspects of this presentation are dependent on Peter Gentry and Stephen Wellum, *Kingdom through Covenant* (Wheaton: Crossway, 2012), chapter 4.

11. Francis Andersen and A. Dean Forbes, *Spelling in the Hebrew Bible,* Biblica et Orientalia 41 (Rome: Biblical Institute Press, 1986) and David Noel Freedman, A. Dean Forbes, and Francis I. Andersen, *Studies in Hebrew and Aramaic Orthography* (Winona Lake: Eisenbrauns, 1992). It seems likely that Ezra had a hand in arranging and editing the books. See Hamilton, 59–63; David N. Freedman, "The Symmetry of the Hebrew Bible," *Studia Theologica* no. 46 (1992): 83–108; Stephen Dempster, "An 'Extraordinary Fact': Torah and Temple and the Contours of the Hebrew Canon: Parts 1 and 2," *Tyndale Bulletin* 48.1-2 (1991): 23–56, 191–218.

12. Peter Gentry and Stephen Wellum, *Kingdom through Covenant: A Biblical-Theological Understanding of the Covenants* (Wheaton, IL.: Crossway, 2012), chapter 4.

13. Wegner, *The Journey from Texts to Translations*, 43–47.

14. One example may be found in 2 Maccabees 12:38-46. According to the apocryphal 2 Maccabees, Judas Maccabee ordered sacrifices to be offered for the sins of slain soldiers who died while wearing pagan amulets, which contradicts the teaching of the canonical Scriptures that repentance or restitution for sin after death is not possible (Hebrews 9:27).

15. 2 Maccabees 7:1-40.

16. From the table of contents preceding the Apocrypha in Martin Luther's translation of the Bible into German: "Apokryphen. Das sind Bücher, so nicht der heiligen Schrift gleich gehalten, und doch nützlich und gut zu lesen sind." Garrick Bailey assisted in this portion of the research.

17. Jude (1:4-6, 9, 13, 15) may have drawn from such texts as *Book of Enoch, Apocalypse of Moses*, and *Testament (Assumption) of Moses* (see Origen of Alexandria, *De Principiis*, 3:2:1). The author of Hebrews (11:37) may have alluded to *Martyrdom of Isaiah*. Paul also quoted pagan authors such as Epimenides (*Kretika*, lost text) in Titus 1:12-13 and Menander (*Thais*, 2:18) in 1 Corinthians 15:33, as well as Epimenides and Aratus (*Phaenomena*, 5) in Acts 17:28.

18. The proper definition of "pseudepigrapha" constitutes an ongoing discussion in biblical studies. See, e.g., Peter Flint, "Noncanonical Writings in the Dead Sea Scrolls," in *The Bible at Qumran*, ed. Peter Flint and Tae Hun Kim (Grand Rapids: Eerdmans, 2001).

19. Josephus, Φλαΐου Ἰωσήπου περὶ ἀρχαιότητος Ἰουδαίων, 1: (8) 41.: "πίστεως δ᾽οὐχ ὁμοίας ἠξίωται τοῖς πρὸ αὐτῶν διὰ τὸ μὴ γενέσθαι τὴν τῶν προφητῶν ἀκριβῆ διαδοχήν."

20. Josephus mentioned a twenty-two-book count of authoritative texts (Φλαΐου Ἰωσήπου περὶ ἀρχαιότητος Ἰουδαίων, 1: [8] 41). His count included the same texts as the twenty-four-book canon; the only difference is that Ruth was included in Judges and Lamentations was included as an appendix to Jeremiah.

How We Got the New Testament

1. Eusebius of Caesarea, *Historia Ecclesiastica*, 6:12:4: "εἰ τοῦτό ἐστιν μόνον τὸ δοκοῦν ὑμῖν παρέχειν μικροψυχίαν, ἀναγινωσκέσθω."

2. In previous writings such as *Misquoting Truth* and *Conspiracies and the Cross*, I [Timothy Paul Jones] have taken the position that the controversy at Rhossus was a conflict in which some at Rhossus wanted to read *Gospel of Peter* publicly, in services of worship, as an authoritative apostolic text—in the sense that would later be described as "canon." After carefully translating and working again through the portion of Serapion's letter preserved by Eusebius of Caesarea, I am inclined toward the conclusion that this was not a conflict over which texts to recognize as authoritative

(in later terms, "canonical"), but over which retellings of events from the life of Jesus were permissible for Christians to receive for the purposes of personal devotion and inspiration. For further discussion, see chapter 4 in C. E. Hill, *Who Chose the Gospels?* (New York: Oxford University Press, 2010) but see also Martin Hengel, *The Four Gospels and the One Gospel of Jesus Christ* (Norwich: SCM, 2000), 12-15. It does still seem to me that *Gospel of Peter* preserves a version of the passion and resurrection that is independent of any account in the canonical Gospels and epistles.

3. Eusebius of Caesarea, *Historia Ecclesiastica,* 6:12:6: "τὰ μὲν πλείονα τοῦ ὀρθοῦ λόγου τοῦ σωτῆρος, τινὰ δὲ προσδιεσταλμένα."

4. It is assumed here that Papyrus Cairo 10759 and Papyrus Oxyrhynchus XLI 2949 represent portions of the text that Serapion of Antioch referenced. It is possible, though less certain, that further portions of *Gospel of Peter* are preserved in Papyrus Oxyrhynchus LX 4009.

5. Papyrus Cairo 10759: "Και ηνεγκον δυο κακουργους και εσταυρωσαν ανα μεσον αυτων τον κυριον αυτος δε εσιωπα ως μηδενα πονον εχων."

6. In *Lost Christianities,* skeptical scholar Bart Ehrman claims, "Serapion concluded that because the book was potentially heretical, it must not have been written by Peter—operating on the dubious assumption that if a text disagreed with the truth as he and his fellow proto-orthodox Christians saw it, then it could not possibly be apostolic" (New York: Oxford University Press, 2003), 16. However, the text from Serapion as preserved in Eusebius's *Historia Ecclesiastica* reveals Ehrman's interpretation to be far more dubious than Serapion's supposed assumption. That to which Serapion compared *Gospel of Peter* was not merely "truth as he and fellow proto-orthodox Christians saw it," as Ehrman claims; Serapion was in possession of copied texts that were known to have been "handed down" from "Peter and the other apostles." When he compared *Gospel of Peter* to these writings, he rightly recognized that *Gospel of Peter* contradicted these writings and thus must have been "falsely ascribed" (ψευδεπίγραφα) to Peter. The writings "handed down" from previous generations were recognized to have come from particular named or known first-century authors; thus, suspect writings were rightly compared to the standard of these earlier writings that were known to have derived from known apostles and eyewitnesses.

Chapter 4

1. Bart Ehrman, *Peter, Paul, and Mary Magdalene* (New York: Oxford University Press, 2006), 259; Bart Ehrman and William Lane Craig, "Is There Historical Evidence for the Resurrection of Jesus?" (March 28, 2006): Retrieved August 1, 2006, from http://www.holycross.edu/departments/crec/website/resurrection-debate-transcript.pdf.

2. Reza Aslan, *Zealot* (New York: Random House, 2013), xxv-xxvi. See also Stephen Patterson, *The God of Jesus* (New York: Bloomsbury, 1998), 214. Of course, most would agree that the New Testament Gospels are not "history," if that term is narrowly defined according to a particular Greco-Roman literary genre; a broad range of scholars agree that the New Testament Gospels are subtypes within the larger literary category of *bios* ("life"). The question here is not primarily one of literary genre, however; it is

whether the New Testament Gospels accurately reported actual happenings in history. It should be noted that significant differences separate Bart Ehrman's perspective on the historicity of the New Testament Gospels—as documents with historical value which originated in the prophetic proclamation of Jesus, a first-century Jewish prophet who announced an impending divine kingdom, who anticipated a soon-coming Son of Man, and whose followers believed him to have been raised from the dead—from Reza Aslan's somewhat more selective and skeptical treatment that concludes Jesus was crucified as a Jewish Zealot; both of these perspectives are distinct from Stephen Patterson, who dismisses the historicity of the New Testament Gospels and locates the meaning of Jesus' life and teachings in the continuing experiences of the community of Christ wherein there was a "resuscitation of hope" that occurred by means of the community's belief that Jesus had been correct about the nature of God (*The God of Jesus,* 239). What each one of these scholars shares, however, is a rejection of the reliability of the New Testament Gospels in the Gospels' report of phenomena such as the miracles and the physical resurrection of Jesus.

3.   Bart Ehrman, *Jesus: Apocalyptic Prophet of the New Millennium* (New York: Oxford University Press, 1999), 47, 52. See also Bart Ehrman, *Jesus, Interrupted* (New York: HarperOne, 2009), 146–147.

4.   For dates of the Galatian and Thessalonian correspondence, see Andreas Köstenberger, et al., *The Cradle, the Cross, and the Crown* (Nashville: B & H, 2009), 413–418, and, Leon Morris, *The Epistles of Paul to the Thessalonians* (Grand Rapids: Eerdmans, 1984), 21.

5.   For estimates of ancient literacy rates and discussions of the impact of illiteracy on modes of communication, see William Harris, *Ancient Literacy* (Cambridge: Harvard University Press, 1989), 326–331; Catherine Hezser, *Jewish Literacy in Roman Palestine* (Tübingen: Mohr-Siebeck, 2001); Tony Lentz, *Orality and Literacy in Hellenic Greece* (Carbondale: Southern Illinois University Press, 1989), 77; Teresa Morgan, *Literate Education in the Hellenistic and Roman Worlds* (Cambridge: Cambridge University Press, 1999). For a more optimistic perspective on ancient literacy, see A. R. Millard, *Reading and Writing in the Time of Jesus* (New York: New York University Press, 2000), 154–185. The writings of Josephus do suggest that—even in a largely illiterate society—Jewish children learned at least to read the Hebrew Scriptures: "καὶ γράμματα παιδεύειν ἐκέλευσεν τὰ περὶ τοὺς νόμους καὶ τῶν προγόνων τὰς πράξεις ἐπίστασθαι, τὰς μὲν ἵνα μιμῶνται, τοῖς δ᾽ ἵνα συντρεφόμενοι μήτε παραβαίνωσι μήτε σκῆψιν ἀγνοίας ἔχωσι" (*Contra Apionem,* 2:204). Still, even among the literate Greco-Roman classes, written records were frequently seen as supplemental to memorized narratives. "For my own part," one ancient orator commented, "I think we should not write anything which we do not intend to commit to memory." For further references, see Samuel Byrskog, *Story as History—History as Story* (Leiden: Brill, 2002) 116–117.

6.   The term "oral history" should be distinguished from "oral tradition." "Oral history" refers to memorized testimonies circulating while eyewitnesses to the events are still living and accessible; "oral tradition" refers to the circulation of these testimonies after the eyewitnesses are no longer accessible (Jan Vansina, *Oral Tradition as History* [Madison: University of Wisconsin Press, 1985], 28–29). The oral histories that were

incorporated into the New Testament never became oral traditions; oral histories became written records while eyewitnesses to the original events were still accessible, alive, and circulating in first-century churches.

7. It is entirely conceivable, though not certain, that early Christians also recorded these testimonies in wax tablets, notebooks, or other written forms that have not survived. In a first-century Greco-Roman context, Quintilian provided recommendations for how to take notes on speeches and even recommends a notebook for that purpose (*Institutio Oratoria,* 10:3; 11:2). For interdependence of orality and literacy in Jewish contexts, see Martin Jaffee, *Torah in the Mouth* (New York: Oxford University Press, 2001).

8. Anthony le Donne, *Historical Jesus* (Grand Rapids: Eerdmans, 2011), 70.

9. Walter Ong, *Orality and Literacy* 2nd ed. (New York: Routledge, 2002), 34.

10. On community as a maintainer of stability of oral histories and on mnemonic devices as aids for memorizations, see Richard Bauckham, *Jesus and the Eyewitnesses* (Grand Rapids: Eerdmans, 2006), 249–250; Michael Bird, *The Gospel of the Lord* (Grand Rapids: Eerdmans, 2014), 40–42, 79–90; Jan Vansina, *Oral Tradition as History* (Madison: University of Wisconsin Press, 1985), 31. Kenneth Bailey contended that the oral histories of the life and teachings of Jesus were transmitted by means of "informal controlled tradition" in which the community as a whole limited the fluidity of the original proclamation even as the original message was applied and adapted in a variety of life circumstances ("Informal Controlled Oral Tradition and the Synoptic Gospels," in *Themelios* 20 [January 1995]: 4–11). Without discounting the helpful foundation that Bailey and Bauckham have provided, Michael Bird has offered a more nuanced modification, building on the work of James Dunn, which he has termed "Jesus in social memory" (*The Gospel of the Lord* [Grand Rapids: Eerdmans, 2014], 95–111).

11. Richard Bauckham, *Jesus and the Eyewitnesses* (Grand Rapids: Eerdmans, 2006), 290–318; Michael Bird, *The Gospel of the Lord* (Grand Rapids: Eerdmans, 2014), 48–62.

12. The total population of Christians in the Roman Empire during this time was probably less than ten thousand. Sociologist Rodney Stark estimates around 7,530 Christians in the Roman Empire (0.0126% of total population) at the end of the first century AD (*The Rise of Christianity* [Princeton: Princeton University Press, 1996], 3–9). With such a small total population of Christians concentrated in a few cities, it is entirely conceivable that eyewitnesses circulating among the churches could effectively curtail fabrications in oral histories and testimonies about Jesus.

13. The Greek verbs translated "delivered" and "received" in this text were technical terms that typically introduced memorized testimonies or traditions (J. L. Bailey and Lyle Vander Broek, *Literary Forms in the New Testament* [Louisville: WJK, 1992], 84). By pairing these two words, the apostle was preparing his readers to hear an oral history that they already knew.

14. Ehrman, *Peter, Paul, and Mary Magdalene*, 259.

15. Paul consistently drew from shared and known teachings from Jesus, many of which were eventually incorporated into the New Testament Gospels. See, e.g., Romans

14:14=Mark 7:19; 1 Corinthians 7:10–11=Mark 10:11/Matthew 5:32; 19:9/Luke 16:16; 1 Corinthians 9:14=Matthew 10:10/Luke 10:7; 1 Corinthians 11:23–25=Mark 14:22–24/ Matthew 26:26–28/Luke 22:19–20; 1 Timothy 5:18=Luke 10:7.

16. Even an individual as literate as Josephus required literary assistance to compose his works in Greek: "χρησάμενός τισι πρὸς τὴν Ἑλληνίδα φωνὴν συνεργοῖς οὕτως ἐποιησάμην τῶν πράξεων τὴν παράδοσιν" (*Contra Apionem, 1:50*).

17. Silvanus may have been the secretary, the courier, or both secretary and courier for the letter now known as 1 Peter; the wording in 1 Peter 5:12 is ambiguous.

18. Richard Burridge and Graham Gould, *Jesus Now and Then* (Grand Rapids: Eerdmans, 2004), 51; George Eldon Ladd, *The New Testament and Criticism* (Grand Rapids: Eerdmans, 1967), 56; Bruce Metzger, *Manuscripts of the Greek Bible* (Oxford: Oxford University Press, 1981), 17–18.

19. On the interplay between oral performance and written content in the ancient world, see Jocelyn Penny Small, *Wax Tablets of the Mind* (New York: Routledge, 1997), 160–201; H. G. Snyder, *Teachers and Texts in the Ancient World* (London: Routledge, 2000), 191–227; Rosalind Thomas, *Literacy and Orality in Ancient Greece* (Cambridge: Cambridge University Press, 1992), 36–40, 124–125.

20. Tertullian of Carthage, *De Praescriptione Haereticorum*, 36: "Age iam, qui uoles curiositatem melius exercere in negotio salutis tuae, percurre ecclesias apostolicas apud quas ipsae adhuc cathedrae apostolorum suis locis praesident, apud quas ipsae authenticae litterae eorum recitantur sonantes uocem et repraesentantes faciem uniuscuiusque."

21. "Mark's Gospel was written well within the lifetime of many of the eyewitnesses, while the other three canonical Gospels were written in the period when living eyewitnesses were becoming scarce, exactly at the point in time when their testimony would perish with them were it not put in writing," Richard Bauckham, *Jesus and the Eyewitnesses* (Grand Rapids: Eerdmans, 2006), 7.

22. Irenaeus of Lyon as reported in Eusebius of Caesarea, *Historia Ecclesiastica,* 5:8:2–4. For discussion of the connection of this text to Polycarp of Smyrna through Irenaeus, see Richard Bauckham, *Jesus and the Eyewitnesses* (Grand Rapids: Eerdmans, 2006), 35. I take the reports from Irenaeus to represent reliable testimony perhaps originating with Polycarp. Interpretations other than martyrdom for the term translated "departure" are possible, but a circumlocution for the deaths of the apostles remains the most plausible reading. The report from Clement of Alexandria (reported in *Historia Ecclesiastica,* 2:15–16) that Peter approved Mark's Gospel does not necessarily contradict the report from Irenaeus that the Gospel According to Mark was passed on after Peter's death; Irenaeus did not claim that Mark composed the book after Peter's death, only that it was distributed after Peter's death.

23. The practice of issuing a text in two languages in two versions that were distinct without contradicting one another was not unknown in the first century AD. Josephus wrote two histories of the Jewish-Roman War, one in Aramaic and the other in Greek. Similar to Matthew's Gospel, only the Greek version achieved sufficient circulation to survive

to this day. The apocryphal book of Tobit was similarly issued in Greek, Hebrew, and Aramaic editions. For considerations related to multiple versions of Matthew, see Martin Hengel, *The Four Gospels and the One Gospel of Jesus Christ* (London: SCM, 2000), 74. For variant forms of Tobit, see Adolf Neubauer, *The Book of Tobit* (Eugene: Wipf and Stock, 2005). For flexibility of ancient notions of "translation," see George Kennedy, "Classical and Christian Source Criticism," in *The Relationships Among the Gospels,* ed. W. O. Walker (San Antonio: Trinity University Press, 1978), 144.

24. For Luke as traveling companion of Paul, see Colossians 4:14; 2 Timothy 4:11; and, Philemon 1:24 as well as first-person plural pronouns in Acts 16:10–17, 20:5–15, 21:1–18, and 27:1–28:16.

25. A detailed presentation of source theories for the Synoptic Gospels stands beyond the scope of this book. For an introduction to primary possibilities, see Andreas Kostenberger, et al., *The Cradle, the Cross, and the Crown* (Nashville: B & H, 2009), 159–173. The Farrer-Goulder hypothesis (Mark as earliest Gospel in present form, with Luke having used both Mark and Matthew), with the addition of an Aramaic edition of the Gospel According to Matthew chronologically prior to Mark's Gospel and a literary independent Greek Matthew, might account both for the interdependence of the Synoptic Gospels and for the testimonies of early church leaders regarding to origins of the Gospels.

26. The author of Revelation may have been John the apostle or John the elder—both of whom were eyewitnesses of the risen Lord Jesus. For Papias's identification of two eyewitnesses named "John," see Eusebius of Caesarea, *Historia Ecclesiastica,* 3:39:3–4.

27. For further discussion, see Michael Kruger, *The Question of Canon* (Downers Grove: InterVarsity, 2013)*,* 67–76.

28. Sinclair Ferguson, "Inerrancy and Pneumatology," The Master's Seminary Summit: Session 15 (March 2015).

29. Definition draws from multiple sources including Tim Keller, "Vision and Values": http://www.redeemer.com, and, Scot McKnight, *Embracing Grace* (Brewster: Paraclete, 2005), 12.

30. Richard Burridge, *What Are the Gospels?* 2nd ed. (Grand Rapids: Eerdmans, 2004) makes a definitive case that the New Testament Gospels fit into the broader category of Greco-Roman *bios.* That said, the Gospel-writers' understanding of Gospels as a continuation of a storyline that God began in the Old Testament and of Jesus as the antitype of Old Testament characters contributed to the composition of the Gospels as a unique subtype of *bios.* For further exploration of this topic, see chapter 2 in Jonathan Pennington, *Reading the Gospels Wisely* (Grand Rapids: Baker, 2012). On the historiographic nature of the Gospels and limitation of "Gospel" to texts which present the "gospel," see Michael Bird, *The Gospel of the Lord* (Grand Rapids: Eerdmans, 2014), 48–56, 289.

31. Papias of Hierapolis, writing in the first half of the second century about what he experienced near the end of the first century, referred to "Aristion and the elder John" as living eyewitnesses; Andrew, Peter, Philip, Thomas, James, the apostle John,

Matthew, and other disciples seem to have passed away, though close associates of these eyewitnesses were still alive and circulating among the churches (Eusebius of Caesarea, *Historia Ecclesiastica,* 3:39:3–4; see analysis in Richard Bauckham, *Jesus and the Eyewitnesses* [Grand Rapids: Eerdmans, 2006], 15–38).

32. Burton Mack, *Who Wrote the New Testament?* (New York: HarperOne, 1996), 46.

33. Tertullian of Carthage, *De Baptismo,* 17: "Sciant in Asia presbyterum, qui eram scripturam construxit quasi titulo Pauli suo cumulans convictum atque confessum id se *amore Pauli* fecisse et loco decessisse." Jerome claimed that it was John who deposed the author of this text, which would place the writing of *Journeys of Paul and Thecla* in the late first or very early second century (Jerome, *De Viris Illustribus,* 7). It is possible, however, that *Journeys of Paul and Thecla* was written later and that Jerome inadvertently added an incorrect detail to the text in *De Baptismo* to which he refers.

Chapter 5

1. Justin Martyr, *Apologia Prima,* 65–67.

2. Martin Hengel, *The Four Gospels and the One Gospel of Jesus Christ* (Harrisburg: Trinity Press, 2000), 116–118.

3. H. Y. Gamble, *Books and Readers in the Early Church* (New Haven: Yale University Press, 1995), 58-66. For supplementary and alternative perspectives, see Martin Hengel *The Four Gospels and the One Gospel of Jesus Christ* (Harrisburg: Trinity, 2000), 118-120; Peter Katz, "The Early Christians' Use of Codices Instead of Rolls," in *Journal of Theological Studies* 44 (1945); T. C. Skeat, "The Origin of the Christian Codex," *Zeitschrift für Papyrologie und Epigraphik* 102 (1994): 263-268; David Trobisch, *The First Edition of the New Testament* (New York: Oxford University Press, 2000), 19–24, 69–71.

4. Martin Hengel, *Studies in the Gospel of Mark* (Eugene: Wipf and Stock, 2003) 77-84; L. L. Johnson, *The Hellenistic and Roman Library* (Ph.D. dissertation: Brown University, 1984); Mary Pages, *Ancient Greek and Roman Libraries* (M.A. thesis: Catholic University of America, 1963); H. G. Snyder, *Teachers and Texts in the Ancient World* (New York: Routledge, 2002), 178.

5. For Christian usage of the *capsa,* see *Passio Scillitanorum,* 12: "Quae sunt res in capsa vestra?" For composition of the *capsa,* see Pliny the Elder, *Historia Naturalis,* 16:43 (84). The *capsa* was also known as a *scrinium* (Martial, *Epigrammaton,* 1:3).

6. Tertullian of Carthage, *De Pudicitia,* 10.

7. Richard Dawkins, *The God Delusion* (Boston: Houghton Mifflin, 2006), 121.

8. Bart Ehrman, *Lost Christianities* (New York: Oxford University Press, 2003), 3–5.

9. Burton Mack, *Who Wrote the New Testament?* (New York: HarperSanFrancisco, 1995) 287.

10. Dan Brown, *The Da Vinci Code* (New York: Doubleday, 2003) 231–234

11. Michael Kruger, *The Question of Canon* (Downers Grove: InterVarsity, 2013), 70.

12. Hebrews, James, 1 Peter, 2 Peter, and 3 John may have been unknown to the author of the Muratorian Fragment (a late second century document, probably originating in Rome), though it is possible that 2 and 3 John were counted as a single text and that the James and 1 Peter were originally included but dropped out due to a copyist error. G. M. Hahneman—despite, wrongly I believe, dating the Muratorian Fragment to the fourth century—recognizes that James and 1 Peter were probably present in the original document now known as the Muratorian Fragment (*The Muratorian Fragment and the Development of the Canon* [Oxford: Clarendon, 1992], 181.)

13. Bart Ehrman, *Misquoting Jesus* (New York: HarperSanFrancisco, 2005), 36.

14. Quoted in Eusebius of Caesarea, *Historia Ecclesiastica,* 3:39

15. It was, according to Eusebius, from these prophetesses that Papias received some stories about the apostles (Eusebius of Caesarea, *Historia Ecclesiastica,* 3:39).

16. Eusebius, *Historia Ecclesiastica,* 3:39.

17. Polycarp of Smyrna, *Pros Philippesious Epistole,* 12:1. Although the first of these clauses derives from Psalm 4:4–5, these two clauses appear together only in Ephesians 4:26.

18. "Tertium euangelii librum secundum Lucam. Lucas iste medicus post ascensum Christi cum eum Paulus quasi itineris sui socium secum adsumsisset nomine suo ex opinione conscripsit—Dominum tamen nec ipse uidit in carne—et idem prout assequi potuit: ita et a natiuitate Iohannis incepit dicere. Quarti euangeliorum Iohannis ex discipulis" (adapted from original Latin).

19. Eusebius of Caesarea, *Historia Ecclesiastica,* 5:8.

20. Irenaeus of Lyon, *Adversus Haereses,* 3:11:8; for Irenaeus as student of Polycarp, see Eusebius of Caesarea, *Historia Ecclesiastica,* 5:20.

21. Ehrman, *Lost Christianities*, 235.

22. This is not to suggest that P52 was titled or ascribed to a particular author; the fragment represents a portion of papyrus too low on the page to know whether any title was present at the top of the page in the original copy. The point here is, rather, to demonstrate the broad geographic distribution of the Gospels at the time when titles probably began to be placed on the manuscripts, which precludes the possibility of names being fabricated later since the result would have been not merely variant *forms of titles* but variant *ascribed authors* for the New Testament Gospels.

How the Bible Made It From Manuscripts to You

1. Two manuscripts from this time period—P75 and P4/P64/P67—were codexes that included all four Gospels together. P45 is somewhat later but included all four Gospels and Acts. It is also conceivable that *libri* refers to Old Testament texts. P46 included the

writings of Paul—with Hebrews but without the Pastoral Epistles—in a single codex.

2. Eusebius of Caesarea, *Historia Ecclesiastica,* 8:2:4: "τὰς δὲ γραφὰς ἀφανεῖς πυρὶ γενέσθαι προστάττοντα."

3. Dana Robert, *Christian Mission* (Hoboken: Wiley-Blackwell, 2009), 26.

Chapter 6

1. This chapter was written by Elijah Hixson with additions by Timothy Paul Jones.

2. Quoted in Frederick Kilgour, *The Evolution of the Book* (Oxford: Oxford University Press, 1998), 71.

3. Bart Ehrman, *Misquoting Jesus* (New York: HarperSanFrancisco, 2005), 7, 10–11, 69, 132, 208.

4. See also Daniel B. Wallace, "Lost in Transmission," *Revisiting the Corruption of the New Testament* (Grand Rapids: Kregel, 2011), 31–33; Darrell Bock, *Dethroning Jesus* (Nashville: Nelson, 2010), 71.

5. Bruce Waltke, "Old Testament Textual Criticism," *Foundations for Biblical Interpretation*, ed. David Dockery, et al. (Nashville: Broadman and Holman, 1994), 175.

6. It should be noted that, if these English sentences of *scriptio continua* were in the context of a book, one would be able to determine the meaning from the context—and this is also what happened in the ancient world when these manuscripts were read and copied. Readers and copyists were able to determine the right reading by considering the context. These two illustrations are commonly used in introductory Greek classes and also appear in Ehrman, *Misquoting Jesus*, 48.

7. See Bart Ehrman's scholarly work *The Orthodox Corruption of Scripture* (New York: Oxford University Press, 1993). In those relatively few instances where the text has been intentionally altered, it was not primarily heretics altering New Testament texts to fit their beliefs; it was often the orthodox altering texts for the perceived purpose of preventing misuse of the text by heretics. While one may take issue with some of Ehrman's specific applications, his overall case is well-argued.

8. Ehrman, *Misquoting Jesus*, 90.

9. Ehrman (*Misquoting Jesus*, 89) places the high end of his estimate at 400,000. Careful statistical analysis by Peter Gurry has resulted in an estimate between 500,000 and 550,000, not including misspellings ("Demanding a Recount," presentation, Evangelical Theological Society, 2014).

10. The listing in 2003 included a total of 5,735 manuscripts of the Greek New Testament represented in whole or in part (Bruce Metzger and Bart Ehrman, *The Text of the New Testament* 4th ed. [New York: Oxford University Press, 2005], 50).

11. K. Martin Heide, "Assessing the Stability of the Transmitted Texts of the New Testament and *The Shepherd of Hermas,*" *The Reliability of the New Testament,* ed. Robert Stewart (Minneapolis: Fortress, 2011), 138. This percentage coheres well with

the seven percent figure for variants suggested by Paul Wegner, *A Student's Guide to Textual Criticism of the Bible* (Downers Grove: InterVarsity, 2006), 231.

12. Wallace, "Lost in Transmission," 20–21.

13. Quoted in F. F. Bruce, *The New Testament Documents: Are They Reliable?* (Downers Grove: InterVarsity, 1972), 20.

14. Ed Komoszewski, M. James Sawyer, and Daniel B. Wallace, *Reinventing Jesus*, Grand Rapids: Kregel, 2006), 82.

15. This presentation is based on Reuben Swanson, ed., *New Testament Greek Manuscripts: Variant Readings Arranged in Horizontal Lines Against Codex Vaticanus: John* (Pasadena: William Carey International University Press, 1995).

16. For an article demonstrating that the pause to re-ink a pen sometimes results in mistakes, see P. M. Head and M. Warren, "Re-Inking the Pen: Evidence from P. Oxy. 657 (P13) Concerning Unintentional Scribal Errors," *New Testament Studies* 43 (1997): 466–73.

17. The first quotation from 1 John that includes these words is found in the writings of Priscillian, near the end of the fourth century. See A. E. Brooke, *A Critical and Exegetical Commentary on the Johannine Epistles* (New York: Scribner's, 1912), 158.

18. Metzger and Ehrman, *The Text of the New Testament* 4th ed., 88.

19. For references to information in this table, see P. W. Comfort and D. P. Barrett, *The Text of the Earliest New Testament Greek Manuscripts* (Wheaton: Tyndale House, 2001); Ehrman, *Misquoting Jesus*, 56; Carlo Maria Martini, *Il problema della recensionalità del codice B alla luce del papiro Bodmer XIV.*, Analecta biblica 26 (Roma: Pontificio Istituto Biblico, 1966); Metzger and Ehrman, *The Text of the New Testament* 4th ed.; Brent Nongbri, "The Use and Abuse of P52," *Harvard Theological Review* 98 (2005) 23–48; Brent Nongbri, "The Limits of Palaeographic Dating of Literary Papyri," *Museum Helveticum* 71 (2014): 1-35; Pasquale Orsini and Willy Clarysse, "Early New Testament Manuscripts and Their Dates," *Ephemerides Theologicae Lovanienses* 88 (2012) 443–474; A. T. Robertson, *An Introduction to the Textual Criticism of the New Testament* (Nashville: Broadman, 1925), 85.

Chapter 7

1. David Norton, *A History of the English Bible as Literature* (Cambridge: Cambridge University Press, 2000), 3. King Henry IV issued *De Heretico Comburendo* in 1401, authorizing burning at the stake as a penalty for possession of Lollard literature, which would have included Wycliffe's Bible (*Documents of the Christian Church,* 3rd ed., ed. Henry Bettenson and Chris Maunder [Oxford: Oxford University Press, 1999], 198–202). In 1408, the *Constitutiones* approved at Oxford forbade even the possession of an English Bible (John Johnson, trans. *A Collection of the Laws and Canons of the Church of England, from Its First Foundation to the Conquest, and from the Conquest to the Reign of King Henry VIII* volume 2 [Oxford: Parker, 1851], 457–474).

2. An early draft of this chapter was researched and written by John David Morrison; Garrick Bailey created an additional draft.

3. F. F. Bruce, *The English Bible* (New York: Oxford University Press, 1970), 2–5; Richard Marsden, "The Bible in English," in *The New Cambridge History of the Bible: From 600–1450*, Volume 2 (Cambridge: Cambridge University Press, 2012), 219.

4. Bruce, *The English Bible*, 6; "Epistola de obitu Bede," *Bede's Ecclesiastical History of the English People,* ed. R. A. B. Mynors, et al. (Oxford: Clarendon, 1969), 582; Paul Wegner, *The Journey from Texts to Translations* (Grand Rapids: Baker, 1999), 276.

5. Marsden, "The Bible in English,", 222.

6. Bruce, *The English Bible*, 8–11; J. I. Mombert, *English Versions of the Bible* (New York: Anson, 1883), 17.

7. Paul Wegner, *The Journey from Texts to Translations* (Grand Rapids: Baker, 1999), 278. The defeat of King Harold II at Hastings was only the beginning of the Norman conquest, of course, which was followed by the proclamation of Edgar the Atheling as a rival king and revolts that continued through 1072 (Marc Morris, *The Norman Conquest* [New York: Pegasus, 2014])—all of which stands beyond the scope of this book.

8. The format of this answer to the question of how the chapters and verses originated is based on a blog post that I [Timothy Paul Jones] read at some point but which I have been unable to locate since that time.

9. Herbert Workman, *John Wyclif,* vol. 2 (Oxford: Clarendon, 1926), 150.

10. Dyson Hague, *The Life and Work of John Wycliffe* (London: Church Book, 1935), 94.

11. Mary Dove, *The First English Bible* (Cambridge: Cambridge University Press, 2011), 17–18.

12. *Writings and Examinations of Brute, Thorpe, Cobham, Hilton, Pecock, Bilney, and Others* (Philadelphia: Presbyterian Board, 1842), 218, 231–232; George Punchard, *History of Congregationalism,* vol. 1 (New York: Hurd and Houghton, 1865), 560.

13. Dove, *The First English Bible*, 6; Matthew Spinka, *John Hus' Concept of the Church* (Princeton: Princeton University Press, 1966), 296–297

14. Margaret Deanesley, *The Lollard Bible* (Eugene: Wipf and Stock, 2002), 296

15. Phillip Schaff, et al., *History of the Christian Church,* vol. 5 part 2 (New York: Scribner's, 1910), 325.

16. Thomas Fudge, *The Magnificent Ride* (Surrey: Ashgate, 1998), 1. This prophecy, at least in the form that Martin Luther later knew it, may have conflated words later spoken by Jerome of Prague with words spoken by Jan Hus.

17. Herbert Workman and R. M. Pope, "Introduction," *The Letters of John Hus* (London: Hodder and Stoughton, 1904), 1.

18. John Wycliffe, *De Veritate Sacrae Scripturae* vol. 1, ed. Rudolf Buddensieg (London: Truebner, 1905), 29.

19. Desiderius Erasmus, *The Correspondence of Erasmus: Letters 1 to 141, 1484–1500* (Toronto: University of Toronto Press, 1974), 252. This quotation about Erasmus' passion for Greek has been unfortunately distorted in modern times into an apocryphal quotation regarding a general passion for books: "When I get a little money I buy books; and if any is left I buy food and clothes." While this is certainly an admirable sentiment—especially if the books you buy happen to be ones I've written—Erasmus did not say it.

20. The 1516 *Novum Instrumentum Omne* of Erasmus was the first *published* Greek New Testament but not the first *printed* Greek New Testament. The Complutensian Polyglot, which included the New Testament in Greek, was printed two years prior to Erasmus' *Novum Testamentum Omne* but remained unpublished until the Old Testament portions of the Polyglot were completed.

21. J. Keith Elliott, "The Text of the New Testament," *A History of Biblical Interpretation,* vol. 2, ed. A. J. Hauser and Duane Vatson (Grand Rapids: Eerdmans, 2009), 241.

22. John Foxe, *The Book of Martyrs* (Hartford: Robins, 1857), 258–259.

23. Timothy George, *Theology of the Reformers,* rev. ed. (Nashville: B&H, 2013), 336–337.

24. David Teems, *Majestie* (Nashville: Nelson, 2010), 228.

25. Andrew Edgar, *The Bibles of England* (London: Gardner, 1889), 59–60.

26. Foxe, *The Book of Martyrs*, 264.

27. The New Testament, the Torah, Joshua, Judges, Ruth, 1 and 2 Samuel, 1 and 2 Kings, 1 and 2 Chronicles, and Jonah in Matthew's Version seem to have been the work of Tyndale. See David Daniell, ed., *Tyndale's Old Testament* (New Haven: Yale University Press, 2002).

28. Adapted from R. Tudur Jones, et al., *Protestant Non–Conformist Texts,* vol. 1 (Eugene: Wipf and Stock, 2007), 108.

29. Alister McGrath, *In the Beginning* (New York: Doubleday, 2008), 161.

30. See in particular the notes in the Geneva Bible associated with Exodus 1:19; 2 Chronicles 15:15–17; and, Daniel 6:22.

31. The King James Version is translated mainly from Erasmus' Greek New Testament via Stephanus and Beza but does not universally agree with any one of the Textus Receptus texts, revealing that the translators did not work from a single text but from several, consulting not only Greek New Testaments but also texts such as the Complutensian Polyglot and the Latin Vulgate. See table in James White, *The King James Only Controversy* (Grand Rapids: Baker, 2009), 104–113.

32. The percentage may be higher. See Jon Nielson and Royal Skousen, "How Much of the King James Bible is William Tyndale's?" *Reformation* 3 (1998): 49–74.

33. D. A. Carson, *The Inclusive Language Debate* (Grand Rapids: Baker, 1998), 72.

34. Isaac H. Hall, *The Revised New Testament and History of Revision* (Philadelphia: Hubbard, 1881), 80, 89.

35. Wegner, *The Journey from Texts to Translations*, 329.

36. James Hamilton, *God's Glory in Salvation through Judgment* (Kindle edition; Wheaton: Crossway, 2010), loc. 13478.

37. Eugene Nida, *Toward a Science of Translating* (Leiden: Brill, 1964), 159.

38. Nida, *Toward a Science*, 160.

39. Wycliffe Bible Translators, "Translation Statistics," http://www.wycliffe.org/About/Statistics.aspx. Accessed 6 May 2014.

40. Athanasius of Alexandria, "Περὶ τῶν θείων γραφῶν," *Quellensammlung zur Geschichte des Neutestamentlichen Kanons bis auf Hieronymus,* ed. Johannes Kirchhofer (Zürich: Meyer, 1844), 8–9

Appendixes

1. Daniel Block, *The Gospel According to Moses* (Eugene: Cascade, 2012), 24.

2. Duane Garrett, "The Undead Hypothesis: Why the Documentary Hypothesis Is the Frankenstein of Biblical Studies," *Southern Baptist Journal of Theology* (2001)

3. For Mosaic-era alphabetic literary productions, see references in Daniel Block, *The Gospel According to Moses,* 49–51. See also Neil Lightfoot, *How We Got the Bible* third edition (Grand Rapids: Baker, 2003), 12.

4. Duane Garrett, *Rethinking Genesis* (Fearn: Mentor, 2000).

Index

Paraphrase 117, 119, 126, 129, 142, 159
Parchment 17, 27, 35
Paul, Apostle 11, 12, 13, 18, 67, 68, 70, 71, 72, 74, 75, 76, 77, 78, 79, 82, 89, 90, 92, 93, 146
Pentateuch. *See* Torah
Peter, Apostle 13, 62, 63, 71, 74, 76, 77, 78, 79, 85, 90, 91, 155
Plato 109, 110
Plenary 147
Polycarp 78, 92, 93, 105
Printing Press 132
Prophets 9, 12, 20, 28, 30, 31, 41, 52, 53, 54, 55, 57, 58, 60, 84, 150, 151
Protestant 49, 55, 137
Pseudepigrapha 58
Puritans 137, 138, 139

Q

Q (Hypothetical Source) 155

R

Received Text. *See* Textus Receptus
Revelation, book of 77, 79, 85, 91, 95, 97, 118, 120
Revised Version 140, 143, 157
Roman Catholic 47, 48, 49, 128, 138, 157
Roman Empire 23, 48, 67, 69, 70, 72, 73, 79, 80, 84, 94, 100, 132

S

Scribes 17, 27, 31, 32, 37, 38, 39, 41, 55, 79, 150, 151
Scriptio Continua 107
Scriptures. *See* Bible
Scrolls 10, 30, 35, 38, 39, 42, 44, 55, 56, 74, 84, 85, 105
Septuagint 30, 47, 48, 56, 57, 58
Serapion 62, 63
Shepherd, The 85, 86, 120
Silvanus 74, 75, 76
Solomon, King 14, 30, 32, 49
Sosthenes 75
Speratus 100

Stephanus (Estienne), Robertus 127, 133, 134
Sufficiency of Scripture 7, 11, 15, 16, 17, 18, 106, 109

T

Tanak 56
Ten Commandments 28, 29, 52, 130
Tertius 73, 74, 75
Tertullian 10, 15, 24, 74, 86
Testaments, Old and New
  Comparison 22, 24, 27
  Definition 10, 28
Textual Criticism 39, 40, 106, 107
Textus Receptus 134
Torah 29, 30, 35, 36, 41, 43, 52, 60, 149, 150, 151
Translation. *See* Bible
Tyndale's Translation 135, 138, 140, 143
Tyndale, William 101, 133, 134, 135, 136, 137, 138, 139, 140, 141

U

Uncial Script 115

V

Valentinus 155, 156
Variants 17, 107, 108, 109, 110, 111, 114, 116
Verbal-Plenary Inspiration 12, 147. *See also* Inspiration
Vulgate 48, 125, 127, 129, 132

W

Wellhausen, Julius 149
Wessex Gospels 126
Wycliffe Bible 129, 130, 132, 137, 140, 143
Wycliffe, John 101, 128, 129, 130, 132

Y

YHWH 149, 151